HISTORIC HOMES
OF T•E•X•A•S

HISTORIC HOMES
OF T•E•X•A•S

Across the Thresholds of Yesterday

Ann Ruff and Henri Farmer

Lone Star Books
A Division of Gulf Publishing Company
Houston, Texas

HISTORIC HOMES OF TEXAS

Library of Congress Cataloging-in-Publication Data

Ruff, Ann, 1930–
   Historic homes of Texas: across the thresholds of yesterday/Ann Ruff, Henri Farmer.
      p. cm.
   Includes index.
   ISBN 0-88415-332-0
   1. Dwellings—Texas—Guide-books. 2. Historic buildings—Texas—Guide-books.   3. Architecture, Domestic—Texas—Guide-books.
4. Texas—History, Local.   5. Texas—Description and Travel—1981—Guide-books.   I. Farmer, Henri.   II. Title.
F387.R835 1987   87-19393
917.64′0463—dc19   CIP

ISBN 0-88415-332-0

❖ CONTENTS ❖

THE GULF COAST _____ 37

Let Lone Star Books show you the best of Texas:

Ray Miller's *Eyes of Texas® Travel Guides:*

Dallas/East Texas, 2nd Edition (Available January 1988)

Fort Worth/Brazos Valley

Hill Country/Permian Basin

Houston/Gulf Coast, 2nd Edition

Panhandle/Plains

San Antonio/Border

Ray Miller's *Houston*

Ray Miller's *Texas Forts*

Ray Miller's *Texas Parks*

The Alamo and Other Texas Missions to Remember

Amazing Texas Monuments and Museums

Backroads of Texas/2nd Edition

Beachcomber's Guide to Gulf Coast Marine Life

The Best of Texas Festivals

Bicycling in Texas

Camper's Guide to Texas Parks, Lakes, and Forests/2nd Edition

From Texas Kitchens

Frontier Forts of Texas

Great Hometown Restaurants of Texas

A Guide to Fishing in Texas

A Guide to Historic Texas Inns and Hotels/2nd Edition

A Guide to Hunting in Texas

A Guide to Texas Lakes

A Guide to Texas Rivers and Streams

Hiking and Backpacking Trails of Texas/2nd Edition

Historic Homes of Texas

A Line on Texas

Rock Hunting in Texas

Texas Birds: Where They Are and How to Find Them

Texas—Family Style

Traveling Texas Borders

Unsung Heroes of Texas

Why Stop? A Guide to Texas Historical Roadside Markers/2nd Edition

❖ DEDICATION ❖

To Melissa Lewis Beck, a great editor and friend
Ann Ruff

To Delores Keller and Gail Drago who encouraged me to write
Henri Farmer

❖ PREFACE ❖

Texans have preserved an abundance of grand, ornate, and majestic old homes. Even a number of humble log cabins and modest frame dwellings have withstood the onslaught of progress. Often the houses are surrounded by glass and steel skyscrapers or perhaps seedy neighborhoods, but there they are—still standing as a reminder of Texas' heritage.

It was rewarding to find that towns and cities over our state are restoring these tangible reminders of the past. In most cases civic organizations and heritage societies have preserved the homes and mansions of their respective towns and cities; in other cases diligent individuals have done their share by personally restoring and endowing these remnants of Texas history. It was a pleasure to work with all the persons involved in restoration and to share in their enthusiasm for their project. We are deeply indebted to all the dedicated people whose restoration efforts made this book possible.

Clearly, it was impossible to include every historic home in Texas, so we limited our choices to those open to the public. Even then we had to keep our stories and selections within workable limits. This was difficult; some homes are worthy of a book on their architecture and furnishings alone, and in other instances the lives of many of the men and women who lived in these homes merited a volume of their own. So, with the limitations of space, we told their stories, which we hope will encourage visitors to tour these wonderful sites and envision the way earlier generations of Texans lived. Here in *Historic Homes of Texas* we have presented an insight into the lives of great and memorable Texas personalities and the contribution they and their homes made to the development of our unique state.

Ann Ruff
Henri Farmer

NORTHEAST
AND EAST TEXAS

Sam Rayburn House

Among the famous Texans who loved the common man and preferred a simple life himself was Samuel Taliaferro Rayburn, the U. S. Congressman who served 25 consecutive terms from the 4th district. Throughout his 48-year career in Congress, this famous and powerful Texan never lost touch with his rural beginnings. Whenever he could, he came back to his lovely home place in Bonham and to the people and the pleasures of the farm and ranch work he loved. Three years after his election to Congress, Sam built a frame house for his parents, but he already had a grander one in mind. He wrote to a friend in 1916, "I am very happy that I have a position with enough compensation that I can save a good deal of money and take good care of my parents and loved ones. I am starting now to build us a nice house on a splendid farm we have bought just two miles west of Bonham." When his plans were realized, the house became the unpretentious and comfortable home for not only the celebrated Speaker of the House but also for many family members; relatives who dwelt in the home for varying periods of time were his parents, sister Lucinda, brother Tom, sister Meddie Rayburn Bartley and son, a cousin from Tennessee, brother Will, and later sister Meddie again with her husband. Although the "Home Place" was improved over the years to make it comfortable, the Rayburn lifestyle remained simple and modest.

The downstairs sitting room still has Sam's favorite wooden rocking chair beside the fireplace, a photo of his parents, and the day bed on which he received guests. In the more formal parlor hangs a Salinas bluebonnet painting, a gift from Sid Richardson. The nicest furniture in the house is in the room of sister Lucinda who served as Congressman Rayburn's hostess in Washington. The twelve-room home gives the feeling that the Speaker or other family members have just stepped out and will return shortly. Even Rayburn's well-worn boots and saddle are close at hand, and a gavel rests on a sturdy desk as if he will call his fellow congressmen into session again at any moment.

Rt. 3, Box 308
Bonham 75418
214-583-5558
Hours: 10:00–5:00, Tues. through Fri.
1:00–5:00, Sat.
2:00–5:00, Sun.
Free admission

The spacious Sam Rayburn Home has been preserved in such an original state that one gets the feeling the family will return any moment.

Downes-Aldrich House

206 N. 7th St.
Crockett 75835
409-544-4804
Hours: 2:00–4:00, Sat. and Sun.
*   Closed Jan. and Feb.*
Admission charge

If you wanted some ideas on how to design your Victorian home, a smart idea was to order an 1895 issue of *Artistic Homes*. This "beautiful illustrated book of residence designs will tell you how to plan and build them" and notes that it "will make you familiar at once with the latest ideas and styles." Selling this wealth of knowledge for the bargain price of four cents, was the firm of George F. Barber and Company, Architects, Knoxville, Tennessee. (The firm still exists today as Barber and McMurry, Inc.) James Elbert Downes of Crockett obviously bought a copy of *Artistic Homes* for he ordered a set of Barber's plans. Even though Downes made substantial changes from these original plans, a photograph shows that the exterior corresponds very closely to Barber's design.

James Elbert Downes was a colonel in the Civil War and born in Yazoo City, Mississippi. When he arrived in Crockett he became a successful merchant and active civic leader. His fortune had prospered to the point that he could afford the lavish fittings and millwork still in evidence in the house. The rare curly pine woodwork was shipped from his native state. Downes married Lizzie Brown and they had three sons. Edward, their youngest son, was killed while serving in the army in the Philippines in 1901, and Lizzie never recovered from her grief. Downes offered the house for sale in 1910 and moved to Dallas.

Crockett's Downes-Aldrich Home is a Victorian masterpiece of turrets, gables, porches, and gingerbread—all from a $6,000 catalog order.

Armistead Albert Aldrich purchased the house in 1911 for his wife Willie and their six children. Aldrich was extremely active in local politics and became a highly respected judge.

Barber's plans were wonderful, for this house is a Victorian masterpiece. For $6,000 Downes got turrets, gables, porches and gingerbread. Inside, four fireplaces use only one chimney, and the popular bullseye woodwork is a traditional dark brown, as are the inside shutters.

Most of the rooms are in the process of being furnished, and some wonderful pieces are already in the house. Crockett families and organizations have picked a room to refurbish, and the slow and costly process of bringing the home back to its former beauty is well underway.

(See color photo.)

DeGolyer Estate (Rancho Encinal)

The rags to riches story of Everette DeGolyer began in a sod house in Kansas and ended in one of Texas' most magnificent mansions. His was a real-life Horatio Alger story.

This brilliant geologist truly had the Midas touch. In 1910, DeGolyer at age 24 was working his way through college as a field geologist near Tampico, Mexico. He picked his first well locations on a hunch, and his brilliant educated guess brought in one of the largest oil wells the world has ever known. *Porero del Llano #4* produced the incredible total of 130 million barrels of oil before it became a dry hole eight years later. Young DeGolyer was a millionaire before he finished college.

History called DeGolyer the "father of geophysical exploration," and his list of accomplishments boggles the mind. This genius formed the most renowned petroleum consulting service in the world. His amazing work as Deputy Petroleum Administrator and advisor to the Atomic Energy Commission made him the most respected authority on natural resources for three presidents. Mr. De of Texas, as he came to be known, also amassed one of the most notable book collections in existence. But, Mr. De often said he was most proud of his position as chairman of the board of the *Saturday Review of Literature*.

After his graduation from the University of Oklahoma, DeGolyer married Nell Goodrich and took her back to Mexico until the Revolution of 1914. In the States success after success followed DeGolyer's brilliant career. He pioneered new drilling equipment and discovered a major strike at the Edwards Oil Field in Oklahoma. Volumes could be written about DeGolyer's technical accomplishments, even to founding Geophysical Services, Inc., the forerunner of Texas Instruments.

The DeGolyers moved to Texas in 1936, and in 1939 purchased property on White Rock Lake in Dallas. *Rancho Encinal* was to be a hacienda reminiscent of their life in Mexico. It was to "look 100 years old upon completion." The result is a rambling one-story 13-room mansion (plus 7 baths), 235 feet in length. This Spanish Colonial Revival house is of soft white stone and stucco accented by a red tile roof and took a year to build. Innovations such as fluorescent light and cen-

8617 Garland Road
Dallas 75218
214-327-8263
Hours: March–Oct.: 10:00–6:00,
Tues.–Sun.
Nov.–Feb.: 10:00–5:00,
Tues.–Sun.
Admission charge (free for all visitors
on Tuesdays)

tral air conditioning were included, guaranteed to make the rest of the Dallas millionaires envious.

The foyer, living room, and dining room are reminiscent of baronial halls of old English mansions. These rooms hosted a steady stream of famous scientists, bankers, publishers, and heads of state. The heavy hammered silver and glass Spanish chandelier in the foyer was a gift to a parish church in Fonseca, Spain, from a Castillian nobleman in 1704. Each medallion in the heavily coffered ceiling of rose and camphor leaf design was hand-poured.

Mr. De was such an avid collector of books his library, which forms the heart of the mansion, is about the size of a two-bedroom apartment. The floor-to-ceiling bookcases once contained 15,000 volumes, and two secret rooms behind sliding bookcases stored his rarest and most precious books.

In addition to collecting rare and priceless books, the DeGolyers collected Indian, Mexican and Pre-Columbian art. These prize objects were displayed in the adobe-styled Indian Room. Used for casual gatherings, its thick orange walls and hewn beam ceiling created the atmosphere of the American Southwest.

Much of the furnishings have been removed by the DeGolyer children, but photographs depict the grandeur of *Rancho Encinal* when the DeGolyers were alive. The few pieces left are of the Spanish design they loved so much.

When the mansion was finished, a master landscape design was also completed. Mrs. De loved flowers and had a special flower room for creating her arrangements. Here on the estate formal European gardens with statues, fountains, and boxwood blend with landscapes and woodlands of natural plants. A long magnolia *allee* and several vegetable and cutting gardens are also part of the exquisite landscaping.

Dallas has completely surrounded the old dairy farm that became the fabulous DeGolyer Estate, but it still remains an island of peaceful beauty shielded from the hectic rush of Dallas traffic. What a magnificent tribute Mr. De left his adopted state and his home reflects the life of a man who greatly enriched his country by his ingenuity and genius.

(See color photo.)

Old City Park

1717 Gano
Dallas 75215
214-421-7800
Hours: 10:00–4:00, Tues–Fri.
1:30–4:30, Sat. and Sun.
Admission charge

Scattered over the Lone Star State are numerous collections of old homes and ancient buildings that have somehow escaped the demolition crews, and "progress" has passed them by. Many have been moved from their original site, but they are still intact in a welcome environment preserving the Texas heritage. One outstanding group is Dallas' Old City Park operated by the Dallas County Heritage Society. The Society was formed in 1966 to prevent the destruction of Millermore, the largest remaining antebellum home in Dallas.

When William Brown Miller of Missouri arrived in Texas in 1847 with his second wife and five children, his 1,200 acres were in the heart of what is now the posh Oak Cliff subdivision of Dallas. Miller's first home for his growing family was the rude log cabin here at Old City Park. The pioneer was certainly an ad-

William Brown Miller began his Texas career in this crude log cabin in the heart of what is now the posh Oak Cliff Subdivision in Dallas.

vanced thinker for his age, for he wanted his seven daughters to have an education. Some of his neighbors felt the same way, so this determined Texan began a school in this tiny one-room hovel. At one time, the teacher and 13 children were housed in the narrow loft of the cabin.

Texas was good to Miller and by 1856 he began construction of his Greek Revival "mansion." The Civil War interrupted his project, and it was 1862 before the home was completed. The second Mrs. Miller had died and all she would ever know of Texas was her primitive log cabin.

The pillars were originally slender posts, but Miller's daughter later added the Doric columns and the balcony. Except for two mirrors and a day bed, all of the furnishings are donations. Miller is supposed to have taken a nap every day after

After the Civil War William Brown Miller moved from his log cabin to this handsome Greek Revival Mansion.

The 1865 Gano House in Dallas' Old City Park had a "splendid" addition of a bedroom and dining room.

the noon meal on this rather short bed, but at 6 foot-2 inches tall, he probably did not rest comfortably.

On down the narrow gravel path of the Park is the 1845 Gano Cabin. When the house was discovered it had been totally enclosed in a modern facade and looked just like any ordinary house. Now it has been restored to its original construction of two rooms with the "splendid" additions of a bedroom and dining room.

The 1900 George House was rescued from downtown progress in Plano and given a place of honor in Dallas' Old City Park.

The 1900 George House was rescued from downtown Plano. This charming Queen Anne Victorian home was extremely modern with its electricity and *inside* kitchen. The kitchen may have been inside, but the bathroom was still outside, so total modern conveniences were not the order of the day after all.

Note the many typical Victorian characteristics of the construction with the asymmetrical use of gables, decorative scrolled brackets under the eaves, elegant chimneys, and tin-shingled roof. The atypical Victorian feature is the light violet paint on the exterior, but this is actually the color the house was originally painted.

Across the way is another wonderful Victorian home that has been furnished as a doctor's office. The funky wallpaper was actually designed in 1900 and found in a Dallas attic.

Finish your tour of this excellent park with a look at the 1906 Shotgun House, so called because you could fire a shotgun from the front door, and the shot would go out the back door without hitting a wall. Introduced in New Orleans, the houses were one room wide and three rooms deep and the homes of the black laboring class. This shotgun house has been authentically furnished and restored by the black organizations of Dallas and represents an important part of Dallas' history.

Perhaps A. C. Greene in his *A Place Called Dallas* has described Old City Park most vividly. "Walking across their floors, peeking into their rooms, using their tools and toys and trivia . . . How people have lived is the basis for how we see life."

(See color photo.)

Eisenhower's Birthplace

Not until World War II headlines brought General Dwight David Eisenhower into public view was the country and even the general himself made aware of the real birthplace of this famous hero. (Ike listed Tyler, Texas, as his birthplace when he enrolled at West Point.) Jenny Jackson, an elementary school principal, remembered an Eisenhower baby named David whom she had rocked in Denison when she was a teenage baby sitter. The curious educator wrote to the general who was unable to confirm her recollection. However, always the disciplined communicator, Ike put the principal in touch with his mother who confirmed the small frame home as the birthplace of her famous son. The modest two-story house remains today in the same location at the corner of Lamar and Day Streets, then as now only a short distance from the railroad tracks. A locally founded group, The Eisenhower Birthplace Foundation, has been unable to retrieve the original possessions, but local citizenry have been generous in furnishing the house with antiques loyal to the 1890s period when the President's family was in residence. The one Eisenhower piece remaining in the house is a lovely old quilt made by Mrs. Ida Eisenhower and her older sons. The coverlet adorns a bed in the very room where Ike was born.

208 East Day
Denison 75020
214-465-8908
Hours: 10:00 to 5:00 daily
Sept. through May
8:00 to 5:00 daily
June through Aug.
Admission charge

Ike, encouraged by Sir Winston Churchill, spent many restful hours painting scenes and favorite people from his past. One effort now hangs in the parlor. Nearby are several family photos, including one of the President's mother when she was Kansas' Mother of the Year in 1945.

Though the President's birthplace is near a railroad crossing and a major thoroughfare, the house and surrounding city block have been turned into a pleasant, quiet park highlighted by a larger-than-life statue of America's most famous five-star general. Any traveler would welcome a few minutes respite from busy activities to reflect over the birthplace and memories of a man whose military and diplomatic genius lead the world through troubled, turbulent years and America into a period of freedom and peace.

(See color photo.)

Eddleman-McFarland House

1110 Penn
Fort Worth 76102
817-332-5875
Hours: 2:00–5:00, first and third
Sunday of each month.
Admission charge

If you were a Fort Worth citizen at the turn of the century and lived on Quality Hill, you were indeed a prominent member of Cowtown's society. Here overlooking the Trinity River were the mansions of Fort Worth's bankers, cattlemen, and oil tycoons. Time has not been kind to Quality Hill, and only two of its magnificent homes remain. Although one is now office building, the other, the Eddleman-McFarland House is open for tours.

This grand old survivor was built in 1899 for $36,000 for George Ball, a Weatherford banker. W. H. Eddleman purchased the mansion from the Ball estate in 1904 for a paltry $25,000. With its turrets, gables, and finials, the house is considered to be one of the finest examples of late Victorian architecture in Texas today. For that perfect outside balance that Victorian architects adored, a stained glass window was installed in a closet.

The Eddlemans doted on their only child, Carrie, and in deference to her parents' wishes, Carrie and her husband, Hays McFarland, moved into the house with them. The family led an aristocratic lifestyle and entertained lavishly. Many galas and parties were staged on the wide front porch. And, as with many rich Texas families, the house was closed during the hot summers while the family went East.

The estate is now owned by the Junior League of Fort Worth, and their goal is preservation of the McFarland House, not restoration. Since Carrie lived here until her death in 1978, the house is in excellent condition. However, it is largely unfurnished with the exception of a few of Carrie's personal possessions. The only major change to the house was the addition of air-conditioning in the 1950s when Carrie's friends refused to come over and play poker in the warm humid game room. The Junior League did not get the bargain Eddleman did: their purchase price was a steep $270,000.

When the house was built for Ball, the very modern invention of Edison electric lights was installed. A sign was found in the attic with the explicit instructions, "Do not attempt to light with a match. Simply turn key on wall by door."

The Eddleman-McFarland House is one of only two remaining homes that stood on what was once Fort Worth's snobbish Quality Hill.

Substantial and ornate woodwork is the most outstanding feature of the house. The heavy coffered ceiling was ordered from a catalog, and this was not unusual for homes of this era. Each room has a different and intricate parquet floor of ebony, mahogany, and pine. In the corner foyer egg (life) and dart (death) trim decorates the moulding and mantle.

Even though the furniture is no longer a part of the house, photographs in each room show how elegantly it was decorated. Carrie had excellent taste, and she loved pink, which she wore at every dinner party. Carrie was also a Dallas Cowboys fan and at 96 went to her first game.

It is the hope of the Junior League that the Eddleman-McFarland House will serve as a "window" on historical events in Fort Worth during the years it was a grand home on Quality Hill.

Thistle Hill

Thistle Hill is the last of the great homes in what was once the finest residential area in Fort Worth. Built in 1903 by the wealthy cattleman W. T. Waggoner, the house was a wedding gift to his daughter Electra and her husband, A. B. Wharton. In 1911 the house was sold to cattle and real estate millionaire Winfield Scott. Scott hired the original architect, Marshall Sangulnett, to implement a massive renovation and design. Scott died in 1912 and never lived in the house, but his wife and young son did occupy the mansion.

Following Mrs. Scott's death in 1938 Thistle Hill began to deteriorate and became a domiciliary for young working women. By 1976 Thistle Hill was on its

1509 Pennsylvania Ave.
Fort Worth 76104
Hours: 10:00–3:00, Mon.–Fri.
Sat. by appointment.
1:00–4:00, Sun.
Contact: Texas Heritage, Inc.
(Same address)
817-336-1212
Admission charge

Ft. Worth's grand old Thistle Hill Mansion was almost razed, but concerned citizens saved it and continue working to restore its former grandeur.

last days and slated for the demolition crew. Fortunately, a group of concerned citizens who loved Fort Worth's history decided to save the grand old lady, and Texas Heritage, Inc., was organized. With a massive fund drive they were able to raise the $250,000 to purchase the mansion and begin work on restoring it to its 1912 opulence.

Over $350,000 has been spent on unseen structural repairs, and just the heating and airconditioning alone cost $250,000. Much interior work remains for Texas Heritage, Inc. All rooms need complete redecorating and repair. When its restoration is finished, Thistle Hill will take its place as one of the loveliest of Texas homes.

To raise money during the Christmas season, Texas Heritage, Inc. stages "Eight Decades of Christmas" and each room is decorated in accordance with bygone eras. On Halloween, Thistle Hill becomes a haunted house, and a constant ongoing drive for funds is conducted for this premier project.

Howard-Dickinson House

*501 South Main
Henderson 75652
214-657-6925
Hours: 1:00–5:00, Mon.–Fri.
Admission charge*

Poised serenely on a gentle hill overlooking Henderson, the Howard-Dickinson house has survived 128 years of hospitality, history, death, and intrigue. Brothers James and David Howard erected the house utilizing their skills as brick masons and carpenters. These stalwart, pioneer men pointed with pride at their iron-reinforced house with its hand-wrought woodwork and first-in-the-area plaster walls. Legend has it that so bold was their pride in their workmanship that the brothers boasted, "God Almightly Himself could not tear down the house because it was so well-built." The story continues that years later during a thunderstorm

lightning struck one of the two-story columns resulting in very little damage. One of the brothers walked out on the upstairs balcony, shook his upraised fist at the heavens, and shouted, "See, I told you so!"

However, in 1967, this house that nature failed to destroy was almost lost to city demolition crews. Machinery waited on the very premises for the third and final city council destruction vote when the protest of 39 local ladies from the Heritage Society found an ear. The savior was David McMahon, a retiree from Sears, who had been instrumental in restoring other worthy old homes. This Irish gentlemen begged a ten-day reprieve from the city fathers and, with the help of dozens of local volunteers and materials donated from his former employer, pushed through the restoration that resulted in Henderson's Hospitality House.

Many interesting discoveries punctuated the restoration and amazed the volunteer workers. For example, scientific analysis revealed the original plaster walls had been made from a mixture of buttermilk, egg whites, and sand. Another lab report verified the legendary blood stains on the south bedroom floor. Local folklore had reported that Pat Howard died on this spot after he was shot by his brother, George, in another part of the house. The reason behind the killing is unclear; today a small carpet covers the yet visible blood stains.

It was from the parlor that the ghost of Mrs. Howard was first sighted entering the door and ascending the stair. According to two ladies who witnessed the sighting, "She disappeared behind the Confederate flag on the stairwell landing." Though Mrs. Howard has not appeared again, she does periodically move pieces of furniture or other objects and frequently turns the light on in the room where her son died. The mysterious "lighting" of the south bedroom happens so often the curator has asked the police, ". . . to stop calling about the light because we can't do a thing about it."

A special Christmas Candlelight tour is conducted the second Saturday in December and a heritage journey on the second Saturday in April. For only $1 more tour guide Jeanette Stewart will include morning coffee or afternoon tea and provide a tour flexible enough to suit any taste. So whether you prefer to examine the unique structure of the old home, hear about the family and local history, or scare up a ghost story or two, Henderson's Hospitality House has something to satisfy any interest.

The T. J. Walling Home and Depot Museum

Henderson boasts a second medallion-marked dwelling, the T. J. Walling home. Texas' best documented log cabin was actually lived in over 100 years and contains totally authentic furnishings. Interesting features of the tiny cabin are the heating/cooking fireplace with crude cooking pots and the authentic spinning wheel which Depot director Susan Weaver competently demonstrates. The rough log walls, once boarded over to give a smoother exterior, are now in their original state except for the windows which were cut through probably about 1845 after

514 North High St.
Henderson 75652
214-657-2261
Hours: 9:00–12:00 and 1:00 to 5:00,
Mon.–Fri.
9:00–1:00, Sat.
Admission charge

The simplicity of the T. J. Walling log cabin causes visitors to reflect in amazement over the stark existence of Texas pioneers.

Texas' first outhouse to be awarded a historical marker is the J. R. Arnold Outhouse; it may well be the first such award in the nation.

the local Caddo Indians were chased off. Other crude period furnishings remind us to be grateful for the comforts we enjoy today.

The Walling home is actually part of The Depot, a historical complex enjoyed by local historical buffs and used as a hands-on educational tool for children. The museum, a restored 1901 Missouri-Pacific depot, contains relics of Rusk County history. This part of the center is especially for children who are encouraged to learn about pirates, Indians, lost treasures, shady deals, fires, brave men, and heroic women. In fact the cotton warehouse part of the building has been transformed into an innovative learning center with 200 activities to encourage children to manipulate, create, and solve problems.

Looking ahead you won't be able to resist continuing around the walkway joining these sites to the J. R. Arnold Historical Outhouse. The three-holer, designed to fit a variety of "behind" sizes, has a window to provide a light for reading, louvered shutters to give the much-needed ventilation, and the correct size lid to fit each hole. No-longer-available gray ironstone buttons punctuate the top of each cover. The widely publicized historical marker, a true prize, is the first to be awarded to an outhouse in Texas and may very well be the first in the nation.

Sam Houston's Home and Park

Few greater heroes exist than Texas' Sam Houston. In the Huntsville park across from the university named for him, two of his local residences await those who would seek a closer look at the quiet rural life and interests of the hero of San Jacinto. The Raven, as Houston was known to his Cherokee friends, migrated from Tennessee to Texas in 1832 in search of land. He bought property near the Trinity River, set up a law practice, and represented eastern U. S. investors in the land business. When Santa Anna invaded Texas, Houston began the first of his battles for the land he loved by answering the call to gather and lead an army to liberate Texas from Mexico. After his San Jacinto victory liberated the territory, General Sam became the first president of the new Republic of Texas. In 1847 after his presidency he returned to his first home and wrote to a friend that he had traded some of his land at Raven Hill for ". . . a bang up place." The property was a woodland setting with a rustic one-room cabin, a short walk from the Huntsville town square.

The Raven found many hours of enjoyment in this home where he listened to his children playing while he whittled and advised his Indian friends who came to camp in the woods nearby. Though the original structure was small, his wife, Margaret Lea, was happy with her new Woodland Home so near her friends and favored activities in the Baptist church. Soon, however, the growing family needed a larger house. With the family slaves as builders and Sam as architect, they added enough rooms to the original house to serve the needs of the larger family and the numerous guests who came to visit and talk Texas politics. Margaret Houston was the consummate hostess to all, except the Indians to whom she never quite became accustomed.

P. O. Box 2054
Huntsville 77341
409-295-7824
Hours: 9:00–5:00, daily except
       Mondays
       Closed major holidays
Donation requested

The house was made of white clapboard with a Greek Revival portico and the customary dogtrot. Docents dressed in 19th-century costumes guide visitors through the parlor pointing with pride to the rosewood piano that belonged to the Raven's granddaughter, Madge Williams Hearne. The marble-topped table is the original on which Houston signed documents and wrote speeches. Though the original bedroom furniture was taken with them to Austin, the pieces displayed reflect what was used in that era. Upstairs is the bedroom where the children slept. As was the custom of that time, the kitchen was separate from the main house. Cast-iron pots used in that period adorn the massive brick fireplace along with a star-shaped pan which formed the fancy cakes that made Margaret Houston famous as a hostess.

Adjacent to the house is Sam Houston's one-room log cabin law office containing two furnishings of his own craftsmanship—a pine desk and a wardrobe-bookcase. The Sam Houston Memorial Museum is also open for those who wish further insight into the accomplishments and contributions of this noble Texas son.

Steamboat House

In 1861, disheartened from Texas' decision to secede from the Union, Sam Houston resigned from his governorship and tried to return to his beloved house in east Texas. Unable to repurchase the Woodland Home, he was forced to settle for the only other property for rent, the Steamboat House. This architectural oddity was built by the president of Austin College as a wedding gift for his son who had seen a steamboat and wanted something that would catch the eye. The bride believed her father-in-law's gift was ugly and refused to live in it. Still in its original form, the house has no windows, only doors that open to the porches on both levels simulating decks. Everything in the house is original except the dining room floor and roof. The rough plank cedar walls throughout the house are painted, and in the master bedroom is a copy of the picture of Santa Anna's surrender to Houston. The chest at the foot of the master's bed was made at the local prison. (In those days people could provide their own lumber and have prisoners make furniture at no charge.)

Sam Houston lived the final two years of his life in this small home. With Texas engaged in war and estranged from the Union, the Hero of San Jacinto believed his dream was over and his life had been in vain. In 1863 already suffering from a cold, he got caught in the rain and developed pneumonia. At 6:15 p.m. on July 26, he died without seeing the end of the Civil War and the return of his beloved Texas to the Union. His desolation seemed complete when he uttered his last words, "Texas! Texas! Margaret!" Sam Houston's funeral was held in the small parlor of the Steamboat House with just the family and a few close friends attending. Though in 1861 Texans temporarily chose to ignore his advice and follow a different path, they have never forgotten the impact of Sam Houston's life and the diligent efforts he made to ensure the Lone Star State's place in history. For the Texas Centennial celebration, Steamboat House was moved to its present location. Texans wanted to enshrine the final home of Sam Houston, a man whose very name became synonymous with his greatest dream—Texas!

The Atkins-Lemmon House

Remember what it was like going to Grandmother's house? You sat in her comfortable rocking chair, smelled coffee or hot chocolate brewing in the kitchen, and listened to the steady ticking of a grandfather clock while you looked through old family photo albums. You felt a warm glow inside from knowing you were in a place where you were really wanted. If you stop to see the historic home of Mrs. Nettie Mae Lemmon and her son Winston, you see invaluable antiques surrounded by an atmosphere of that same kind of warm hospitality.

The simple exterior of this old Greek Revival-style home fails to prepare you for the treasured antiquities housed in every room. The gentleman's bedroom has a hand-carved brown walnut wardrobe, circa 1830, and a dresser with hand carved pulls and sconces on the sides of the mirror for holding small items such as a watch. Without doubt the most interesting piece in the house is an *encoignure*, a rare asymmetrical corner cabinet of unbelievably ornate design, circa 1795. Though the first of these open cabinets held pastries, later ones were designed with mirrors and multiple small shelves to hold figurines and perfume. Sharing the room is a handsome Victorian sofa from the 1850s featuring simple grape carving and cabriole legs finished with casters to lend a charming simplicity.

407 East Walker
Jefferson 75657
214-665-3679
Hours: Call for appointment
Admission charge

The Atkins-Lemmon Home houses a fabulous collection of antique china and furniture.

Mrs. Nettie treasures her quality antique pieces; however, she finds most meaningful family heirlooms which came from both her family and that of her late husband. These special pieces include gold leaf frames with mirrors, a beautifully crafted walnut wardrobe, an unusual sofa and a trunk that belonged to her grandmother, and a hundred year old handmade coverlet.

The Lemmons' antique furniture would warm the heart of any collector, but a special gleam lights Mrs. Nettie's eyes as she points with pride to her extensive display of antique china. Several sets of Flow Blue are included; among them is one set of King Edward VI of England, dating from 1891. A lawyer's bookcase holds another set of china (Don't let Mrs. Nettie hear you call them dishes!) from the 1700s. In virtually every room in the house you will see exquisite figurines, lovely tea services and entire sets of china. Mrs. Lemmon and her daughter, Annette Daigle, enjoy authenticating as much as collecting; thus, they have verified dates and origins on everything. If you have enjoyed Mrs. Nettie's hospitality, why not step across the street to the French Townhouse and enjoy the hospitality of her daughter's family?

The Brownhouse

112 Vale St.
Jefferson 75657
214-665-2310
Hours: By appointment
Theatre Sat. nights

To round off a perfectly satisfying visit to historical Jefferson, try to reserve time for an evening of "Living Room Theatre" and a tour of The Brownhouse, a beautiful French Quarter-styled early Victorian residence. Marcia and Donald Thomas have restored this old commercial building into a townhouse for themselves while reserving the downstairs living room for theatre performances. The exterior of their home has been so authentically preserved you are sure to believe it houses one of its original commercial establishments—bank, antique shop, used furniture store, gambling and domino parlor, reputed bawdy house, tax collector's office, or motor supply store. Your first step inside, however, causes you to smile at the charm of both Mrs. Thomas and her unique restoration achievement.

Records show that back in 1858 the property was sold with a 12-year-old black girl named Ann "to be a slave for life and sound in mind and body." Though no later records show Ann's attachment to the land, the Thomases have experienced a number of unexplained occurrences which brought them to the conclusion their house may be inhabited by a small but friendly "presence."

The land passed through several hands before a brick store house was erected in 1869 by a family of considerable landholdings and prominence. The building was used for 114 years for a variety of commercial purposes until purchased by the Thomases in 1983. Not wanting to disturb the building's aesthetic quality, the contractor raised the lower floor 18 inches and concealed underneath the new wiring, plumbing, and air-conditioning system. In a doorway which originally connected an adjoining building, shelving was built for displays of old Victorian novels and other collectables. A piece of the floor joist from under an 1859 Episcopal church was refinished and added over the fireplace to act as a mantel.

Although quite modern, the galley-style kitchen was covered with 100-year-old flooring salvaged from the old T & P Railway shops torn down in nearby Marshall. Barstool pillows were covered with an old quilt found upstairs during restoration. A squared star pattern from the quilt was duplicated on the fire screen by three Longview artists. Two exterior walls running the length of both stories still retain their original multiple earthtone colors. The only change was the application of a silicone sealant to help preserve the brick through the next 100 years.

Ten-feet-tall front doors, original to the building, were refinished to their primary state. New banisters and railings were made of wood recycled from other parts of the building. The 23 stairs with deep treads remain indented from over 100 years of continuous use. The upstairs parlor is furnished in an eclectic 1930s style and features an antique art deco hanging light fixture from an old jewelry store in Marshall. Mrs. Thomas refinished her grandfather's old upright Philco radio and turned it into a bar that houses antique crystal stem-ware from the period. Throughout the home, thirties furniture and memorabilia have been integrated to provide a delightful dwelling with a super artistic flare.

Following each Saturday evening's theatre performance, Mrs. Thomas invites the small audience to stay for refreshments and a tour through her delightful home. If you can't stay for the Saturday show, call for an appointment to see the house. The Brownhouse and its lovely mistress/actress will be a charming highlight to your visit to historic Jefferson.

Freeman Plantation

To see Freeman Plantation turn off Highway 49, west of Jefferson. When you enter the grounds, park in the private lot and cross over the small stream on a picturesque footbridge built along the exact path that in earlier years was the road to Dallas. Once over the bridge you will be transported back into the time when cotton was king and riverboats steamed along waterways in the Old South. In season, Magnolia blossoms perfume the air to the entry stairway, and six rocking chairs on the second story porch offer a quiet resting place with a splendid view among gentle whispering trees. Welcome to the genteel life of the Old Freeman Plantation.

Tours begin on the lower floor where slaves hand molded the 14-inch-thick brick walls that help retain a comfortable temperature. Exposed ceilings are framed with cypress timbers that were cut from trees lining the river behind the house. Still visible are the rough marks made by hand axes used to square the beams before they were notched and pegged. When the house was built in 1850, the owner, Williamson Freeman, was a cotton and sugar planter and a river freighter. Therefore, this thousand acres along the river was ideally suited for both his interests. Though the house is of the Greek Revival period, Louisiana raised style was used, probably because the owner feared the rising river water.

Hwy. 49 West
Jefferson 75657
214-665-2320
Hours: 2:30–4:00, daily except Wed.
Admission charge

A definite Louisiana bayou influence is reflected in the Freeman Plantation's raised architecture.

Appointments inside indicate a formal lifestyle enjoyed by people of wealth in the 1850s. Two great halls existed to serve as gentlemen's and ladies' parlors. The authentic winged chaperone couches were used during "courting"; the damsel sat on one wing, the young suitor on the opposite, and the chaperone squarely in the middle. For those who doubt this rigid formal behavior, be reminded that in the 1850s in the Old South a gentleman sometimes wore five pairs of gloves per day. He would never touch a lady's hand without his glove on; and, of course, he dared not touch her hand with the same glove that had held the horse's reins.

Post Civil War days saw the end of the old lifestyle, and times even worse than the war era eventually befell Freeman Plantation. For a period of years in the 1920s, the abandoned house was used as a hay barn. The sturdy cypress wood kept it from deteriorating any worse than seen in pre-restoration photos in the back hall. This stately old home was documented by Roosevelt's survey crew to be preserved for its historic and architectural worth and is so listed in the Library of Congress. It has been completely restored and furnished with authentic Victorian antiques of the antebellum period. Many of these furnishings of New Orleans origin, like the Mallard bedroom suite, probably came to the plantation on a riverboat. Enormous though these suites may be, they were all built to break down for transporting by wagon or boat.

Captain J. M. DeWare married the daughter of the second owner of the house in 1867. Though for a period of time the house was out of DeWare hands, it is back in the family. The J. M. DeWare IV family is in residence and warmly welcomes visitors who would care to cross a bridge in time and sample a few memories of life as lived along the river in the days of white gloves, chaperone couches, and King Cotton.

(See color photo.)

This tiny log cabin in Dallas' Old City Park served as William Brown Miller's home, but it was also a schoolroom for his seven daughters (p. 6).

This delightful gazebo in Dallas' Old City Park is a popular spot for weddings (p. 6).

In addition to its outstanding array of restored houses, Dallas' Old City Park also contains a pioneer town (p. 6).

Multiple visits from important pioneers like Sam Houston, Thomas Rusk, and Davy Crockett made the Sterne-Hoya home in Nacogdoches a historical crossroad in early Texas (p. 27).

The plans for the Downes-Aldrich House in Crockett were ordered from a four-cent catalog (p. 4).

Elegant Maplecroft is the main attraction among the historical structures to be viewed at the Starr Mansion site in Marshall. The stylish home is as livable as it was in its early days in the nineteenth century (p. 24).

From these humble beginnings came our thirty-sixth President. The boyhood home of Lyndon B. Johnson can be seen at the Johnson City unit of the LBJ National Historic Park (p. 93).

Texas Highways

Texas Tourist Development Agency

A message to today's youth awaits those who take a few moments to appreciate the humble birthplace of President Dwight Eisenhower in Denison (p. 9).

A stained glass and leaded dome, two-and-a-half-story great room, and bow-and-wreath-design detailing exemplify the special Victorian glitz seen in the Highlands Mansion in Marlin (p. 81).

The Methodist Parsonage at Millard's Crossing is reminiscent of quaint nineteenth-century homes (p. 26).

Texas Parks and Wildlife

G. H. Pape Foundation

A tour of the Earle-Harrison House in Waco is enhanced by a quiet walk among unique water and flower gardens (p. 93).

The Millard-Lee Home, built in 1837, was occupied continuously by a Lee family member in Nacogdoches until 1968 (p. 26).

The Log House, dating from the 1820s, will be an Albert Thomas museum at Millard's Crossing (p. 26).

This old church is part of the Texas heritage presented at Millard's Crossing in Nacogdoches (p. 26).

Mrs. Albert Thomas' grandfather built the Watkins House for the community of Mahl in 1895. It is now part of the Millard's Crossing complex in Nacogdoches (p. 26).

Glen Davis

Historic home buffs with an eye for craftsmanship will appreciate the decorative detailing in the gorgeous Starr Mansion in Marshall (p. 24).

Granbury proudly offers tours of the Daniel House, a Victorian home occupied exclusively by the family of the same name (p. 105).

Texas Parks and Wildlife

Original family antiques and portraits adorn the Starr Mansion parlor in Marshall (p. 24).

R. Reynolds/Texas Tourist Development Agency

Each bedroom in the beautifully restored House of the Seasons in Jefferson contains either the original or correct period furniture (p. 23).

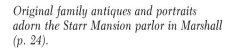

One social highlight during winter in Paris is the Victorian Christmas party at the Samuel Bell Maxey House (p. 29).

Paris Chamber of Commerce

The Daughters of the Republic of Texas manage The Cullen House as a museum and community house in San Augustine (p. 31).

The Freeman Plantation in Jefferson recalls King Cotton days along the Neches River (p. 19).

Egypt Plantation, completed in 1849, is considered one of the finest and oldest Anglo homes in Texas (p. 42).

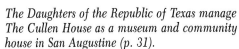

M. Murphy/Texas Tourist Development Agency

Texas Highways

Tyler's Goodman Museum is home to several collections of antique memorabilia belonging to local organizations (p. 33).

San Antonio's King William District has many grand old homes, but the magnificent Steves' Homestead boasted the first swimming pool (p. 91).

Kell House was a central gathering place in the early days of Wichita Falls, and it continues to serve as the frequent venue for parties, annual holiday celebrations, and other social occasions (p. 34).

The French Townhouse

If you enjoyed The Atkins-Lemmon House across the street, you are sure to be enthralled with the French-Gothic architecture of The French Townhouse and an astounding antique collection therein. The entire Daigle family was involved in various aspects of the total restoration before moving into the home in 1975; they have, in fact, made a career of restoration while collecting and authenticating their fabulous antique furniture. The house was designed and construction begun by the son of Jefferson's cofounder; after he died, his brother finished the project. Builders used many local materials but others came by steamers from France via New Orleans and up to Jefferson. In keeping with the house's French flavor, many of the fine antique furnishings were also imported from France and New Orleans. The family room center table is from the workshop of Prudent Mallard of New Orleans. Its ornately carved legs, each bearing different flowers and clusters of nuts, represent the various seasons. Seamstresses will marvel over a massive oak thread cabinet which holds 1,800 spools of thread.

Mrs. Daigle's great decorating courage is shown in her dining room, carpeted in brilliant emerald green and papered with a striking panel design. The dining table is a classic mahogany with chairs from Hickory, N.C., and four ornately carved and mirrored china cabinets from the George IV and early Victorian periods enhance the elegant room. Probably, les pieces des resistances of the house are the furnishings in the sleeping areas. The master bedroom includes an armoire and a triple-mirrored half-tester bed by Prudent Mallard of New Orleans. This renowned craftsman fled France for the freedom to pursue his art in New Orleans. His half-testers were an interpretation of the Lit d'Ange or "angel bed" originally designed for Louis XIV. Queen Victoria gave him an award for producing these beds with self-supporting tops. Then, featured in the guest bedroom is a massive cherrywood, walnut, rosewood, and mahogany three-quarter tester, custom carved by Mallard for Wm. C. Lee, a New Orleans stockbroker and developer. The Daigle collection of antiques is by no means restricted to the exquisite. They take pride in many authentic rustic pieces that belonged to their ancestors and eagerly share them along with items hand-carved by some of Europe's finest craftsmen.

502 East Walker
Jefferson 75657
214-665-2760
Hours: Daily
        Call for appointment
Admission charge

Guarding Oak

Guarding Oak is another of the lovely old antebellum mansions whose former owner played an important Civil War roll; Judge George Todd was a signer of the Ordinance of Secession of Texas in 1861. Jeffersonians might remember him better as the prosecuting attorney in the famous Diamond Bessie murder trial. Nonetheless, his home, Guarding Oak, stands as his memorial after a near century of use. The original story-and-a-half structure was built in 1859. Declining with the fortunes of Jefferson after the city's great days as a river port, the house was even-

301 South Friou
Jefferson 75657
214-665-2345
Hours: 10:00–4:00, Wed. to Sat.
        1:00–4:00, Sun.
Admission charge

tually converted into apartments. A fire dispossessed the tenants and badly damaged the interior of the building but left it structurally sound. Finally, in 1941, Mr. and Mrs. Dan Lester refinished and restored it to its present state of gracious charm.

Surrounded by a brick and wrought iron retaining wall, the house reflects classical architecture representative of an old Southern mansion. Though the original "guarding oak" for which the home was named is gone, green gardens and new oak trees encircle the property. French Victorian furniture, combined with lovely gold wallpaper, lends a regal air to the drawing room; appropriately, the Beehive mark on an Austrian crystal vase indicates it was made for royalty. But in an "Old South" reverie, you can envision the antebellum mistress of the house sitting near her warm fireplace, protected from the heat by the antique beaded petit point fire screen from France. When you step off the drawing room V'sasky carpet, you find yourself in the dining room, where a genuine English Sheraton banquet table of bird cage design, made for royalty and one of five in existence, stands in the center of the room. An exquisite Venetian gas light chandelier and cut glass punch bowl add even more elegance to a breathtaking room lined with high Italian windows and guilded mirrors.

Mrs. Lester taps a centuries-old Japanese gong whose mellow vibrations resound as guests ascend the staircase. Upstairs she conducts you into the bedrooms and points with pride to three antique beds, each of unusual design. The first is a cannon ball bed with matching pieces of solid rock cherry. The button bed in the second room has a secret compartment in a hollow post where in earlier years important documents were probably hidden away. At the foot of the bed is a "convenience piece" holding the chamber pot. Ladies sat on the nearby slipper chair to change their shoes, of course. The third bedroom is home to a Renais-

Guarding Oak was the home of the prosecuting attorney in the famous Diamond Bessie murder trial, a historical tale of intrigue reenacted each year in Jefferson.

sance Revival bed, covered with a quilt made by Mrs. Lester's mother. When the Lesters restored Guarding Oak in 1941, they provided sufficient space and modernization to accommodate the needs of a family. Though modern embellishments have been tastefully added, the last century's elegance and charm have been carefully guarded in the tradition of the old oak that once stood vigilant.

House of the Seasons

A 150 + -year-old Magnolia tree graces the entrance and prepares visitors for antiquity and grandeur inside Jefferson's House of the Seasons. Built in 1872 (Jefferson's heyday of riverboats and railroads), this remarkable mansion combines Greek Revival, Italian, and Victorian architecture to produce a house with its own unique style. The name is taken from its four sided cupola where each wall represents a season of the year with a different color of stained glass. This special floor crowning the top of the house can be enjoyed from three views. The energetic can climb a steep two-flight staircase to enjoy the view from the inside out; the less hardy can gaze up from the grounds into any of the four windows, each of a color representing its season; and all can look up from the entrance hall to view frescoes of maidens dressed in costumes carrying out the four hues in the cupola windows.

The builder and first owner, Benjamin H. Epperson, traveled in the eastern United States after the Civil War and took many of his ideas from eastern influences. Present owners, Richard and Susan Collins of Dallas, enjoy occasional residency in their stately mansion, which they have carefully restored and opened to the public. The Collins are ardent preservationists who purchased their Jefferson

Jefferson 75657
214-665-3141
Tours: 10:30 and 1:30, Mon.–Sat.
1:30, Sun.
Admission charge

A 150 + -year-old magnolia tree shades Jefferson's House of the Seasons and prepares visitors for the antiquity and grandeur inside.

house after it had been vacant for months and was in bad need of repair. Several University of Texas faculty members joined the project to help with the work and provide expertise on period accuracy. Luck was with the Collins in their struggle to authenticate. First, Mrs. Collins discovered some 1880s photos of the house that helped restoration accuracy. Next came the even more surprising discovery that a ninety-five-year-old granddaughter, Jeanie Epperson, was alive and living in a nursing home in Texarkana, only 60 miles away. Susan Collins hastened there, camera and tape recorder in hand, and persuaded the elderly Miss Epperson to share many memories of her childhood in the house and also to give the couple first option on many of the original furnishings that were in storage. Other pieces not original to the house have been painstakingly selected for their loyalty to the period. A noteworthy antiquity is the Knobe Concert Grand built for the 1876 Centennial and played for that occasion in Philadelphia.

Each bedroom contains either the original or correct period furniture, but an 1890 Murphy pull-down bed is sure to capture the fancy of the imaginative. No hint of the bed inside can be seen from the elegantly carved exterior. A favored story recited for visitors to the second floor is of the second Mrs. Epperson who was given the unpopular responsibility of corralling her naughty-for-that-era step-children who loved to frequent the local riverfront saloons. When her repeated warnings failed to halt their late-night, inebriated ascents up the back stairway, Mrs. Epperson had the stairs removed. Granddaughters of the second family to own the home describe playing in the cupola, "a child's paradise." The open stairwell provided a perfect jumping point to the fainting couch below. Children of any age enjoy the secret panel in the stairwell that leads into the attic. Baccarat and Waterford chandeliers testify to the opulence of the house, but the carved marble fireplaces and extensive oriental carpet collection take your breath away. Delighted visitors will marvel at the way the House of the Seasons reflects life as lived back in Jefferson's 19th-century youth of railroads and riverboats.

(See color photo.)

Starr Mansion

407 West Travis
Marshall 75671
214-935-3044
Hours: 9:00–11:00, 1:00–4:00,
Wed.–Sun.
Admission charge

In 1837 the first Starr to immigrate to Texas was Doctor James Harper Starr who settled in Nacogdoches and became active in land and the fiscal affairs of the New Republic. President Lamar appointed him Secretary of the Treasury in 1839, and thereafter he formed a highly successful land agency. Following the Civil War, Starr moved to Marshall where he retired from all business except to manage his own land affairs, considerable by this time. Very soon James Starr bought a large lot with a house called Rosemont, and thus began the large family compound. The oldest Starr son, James Franklin, built Maplecroft for himself, an adjacent school house where his daughters were educated, and eventually houses for them and their families on the same property. With the exception of Rosemont, dismantled in 1914, the entire compound is open for visiting.

The star of the Starr Family State Historic sight is Maplecroft, a lovely, livable old mansion nestled among thirty Maple trees for which it was named. Croft

Maplecroft, the chief attraction in the Starr family compound, enjoys an outstandingly preserved beauty that belies her 106 years.

means nestle—thus the name, Maplecroft. Visitors have a difficult time realizing this grand old mistress of Marshall has passed so many birthdays; she enjoys good looks and a well-cared-for atmosphere that belie her 106 years.

Those enticed by the siren's song of architectural perfection will be amazed at the pains taken to design and create a house to weather time and provide the utmost in comfort for its earliest residents. The New Orleans shipwrights who constructed Maplecroft used only virgin pine completely clear and free of knots. All sills were hewn of oak logs. Between the joists of the 15-foot-high first floor ceiling, the builders used a 4-inch layer of mixed sand, lime, and straw, a unique form of insulation that controlled indoor temperature in extreme weather and made an excellent sound barrier as well. When an east bedroom was added to accommodate the widowed mother of Mrs. Starr, a cellar was dug where drums of gas for generating heat were stored. A windmill pumped the family's daily water needs from a well into a cistern enclosed within the tennis court. Servants checked the cistern level daily to see that sufficient water was available to meet household needs as well as to protect the house in case of fire. A system of speaking tubes still connects several rooms of the house with the kitchen, pointing to the kinds of special conveniences people of wealth enjoyed in the 19th century.

Historic home buffs with an eye for craftsmanship will appreciate the decorative detailing in the house. Fireplace mantles are marbleized iron with cast iron coverings and hearths are of white marble.

Rich family history and pride permeate the house through portraits adorning walls in every room, and the special regard given children remains evident in child portraits and furnishings throughout. The family collection of antique Persian carpets covers all the downstairs floors, but in the summer days before air conditioning, the carpets were replaced with straw rugs. Most of the furniture, some imported from Europe, is the original used by the three grandes dames who presided over this mansion. Each generation has been diligent in modernizing as well as preserving Maplecroft. Even family clothing of several periods was stored in acid proof boxes in an upstairs closet. This glorious and livable old mansion is managed by a Texas Parks superintendent who eagerly invites the public year around. Whether you are a resident or passing through, don't miss the special Christmas Tour held most of the month of December when the old Starr Mansion twinkles brightly as the real star of Marshall.

(See color photo.)

Millard's Crossing

Highway 59 North
Nacogdoches 75961
409-564-6631
Hours: 9:00-12:00, 1:00-4:00,
Mon.-Sat.
1:00-4:00, Sun.
Admission charge

When driving Highway 59 just passed the northern edge of Nacogdoches, a small road forks to the right, crosses the railroad tracks, and enters Millard's Crossing, a marvelous collection of neatly-kept early Texas structures in a serene pastoral setting. Even highway noise and modern Texas evaporate as manicured lawns, white fences, singing birds, and beautiful trees transport you back to an earlier century when life was much less complicated. A total of 16 structures comprise Millard's Crossing, and all but one came directly or indirectly from family connections of Mrs. Albert (Lera Millard) Thomas, benefactress of the settlement. An enthusiastic collector, Mrs. Thomas has moved the buildings to the crossing and furnished them with 19th-century antiques and other personal memorabilia, some of it collected around the world.

The first of the houses, known as the Millard-Lee Home, was built in 1837 by Nacogdoches merchant, Robert F. Millard and was occupied continuously by a Lee family member until 1968. Local citizens must have been relieved when Mrs. Thomas acquired it for restoration in 1970, because even at this late date the house had only one electric light and its privy was behind the Old Fort Bank. Primitive art from well-known Texas artists, Alma Gunter and Billie Stroud, hangs in the dining room, and the guide delights visitors with fascinating interpretations of the paintings. The kitchen has an unusual array of utensils which are a challenge for visitors to identify. Among them are a washing machine with old wooden paddles, an antique mayonnaise maker, and a meat tenderizer. Behind the kitchen is an enclosed porch housing an octagonal hardware cabinet with pie-shaped drawers and a lovely old cash register that would shame any modern computer. A double-entry staircase leads upstairs to a light and airy room filled with antique wicker furniture; large windows allow a beautiful view of the settlement. On the opposite side of the stairway is the document room containing a grand assortment of papers dating from the 1820s to the 1850s.

Another interesting old home in the settlement is the Burrows-Millard House, built as a wedding present by Burrows for his wife whose maiden name was Millard. This home was lived in until 1972 and never left the family's land. Be sure to pass the garage which houses the Cadillac presented to Albert Thomas by President John F. Kennedy the day before he was assassinated. Two other charming edifices open for your enjoyment are a carriage house, holding three antique fire trucks, and an old country church, restored and available to couples who desire a small, intimate and perhaps old-fashioned wedding. As enjoyable as viewing each house in Millard's Crossing is, the stroll through this peaceful community where Mrs. Lera Thomas still resides is even more so. When her husband, the late Albert Thomas, died in 1966, Mrs. Thomas finished her husband's's final term in office (he was first elected to Congress in 1936); thus she became the first congresswoman from Texas. Mrs. Thomas has gone to great pains to restore the settlement of Millard's Crossing and to provide an opportunity for visitors to examine and enjoy an hour's reverie of 19th-century East Texas.

(See color photo.)

Sterne-Hoya House

Around 1830 when Texas was still part of Mexico, Adolphus Sterne built a finely detailed home for his bride, Eva Catherine Rosine Ruff. It is probably the oldest house in Texas which still stands on its original property. Throughout its history, the home became a visiting place for some of Texas' best known citizens. Here, Sam Houston was baptized a Catholic, with Mrs. Sterne as his godmother, so that the future hero of San Jacinto could own land in a Mexican territory. Thomas Rusk, one of the two first United States Senators from Texas, was a frequent guest in the Sterne home; and Davy Crockett, hero of the Alamo, spent a fortnight here in 1836. Charles Taylor, signer of the Texas Declaration of Independence, married Mrs. Sterne's sister in the parlor; and here Chief Bowles of the Cherokee Indians signed a peace treaty. Multiple visits from such important Texas people made the Sterne home almost a historical crossroads.

211 South Lanana
Nacogdoches 75961
409-564-4693
Hours: 9:00–12:00, 2:00–5:00
Closed Sun. and holidays

The Stern-Hoya Home has been decorated to reflect the lifestyles of both families who resided within.

Adolphus Sterne, builder and first owner, became a Scottish Rite Mason, an accomplishment which proved of significant value later. As a landowner in Texas, Sterne had to pledge his loyalty to Mexico; nevertheless, he actively supported Texas' struggle for independence. When Mexican soldiers caught him smuggling firearms, he was tried for treason and sentenced to be shot. Only the intervention of his New Orleans Masonic Lodge brothers saved him. He was released on the condition that he would never again bear arms against Mexico, and Sterne, being a man of honor, "technically" kept his word. He did, however, financially encourage the territory's fight for freedom when he recruited and financed two volunteer companies for the Texas army.

Seventeen years after her husband's death, Mrs. Sterne sold the home to Joseph von der Hoya, a Prussian immigrant, farmer, and large land owner. The double name, Sterne-Hoya, relfects the respect for the times and styles of the two very different families for which the house was named. In an effort to honor both, Nacogdoches historical enthusiasts have succeeded in preserving and decorating two parlors in furnishings typical for each family's era. The Friends of the Adolphus Sterne Home, a non-profit corporation, preserved the old home to its present splendor, and members offer a genuine welcome as they guide visitors through this lovely old home that commemorates Nacogdoches' and Adolphus Sterne's role in Texas struggle for independence.

(See color photo.)

Tol Barret House

Three miles south of Loop 224 near
*   FM 2863*
Nacogdoches
Contact: Captain and Mrs. Charles
*   Phillips*
*   Route 4, Box 9400*
*   Nacogdoches 75961*
*   409-569-1249*
Hours: Appointment only
Admission charge

After winding your way through the beautiful East Texas Piney Woods, you come upon a Texas pioneer cabin that rests on stone block foundations just as it did in another place, another time. Here lived one of the great unsung heroes of Texas, Lyne Taliaferro Barret, or "Tol" as he was affectionately called. Tol Barret made the first oil strike in Texas. (See *Traveling Texas Borders*, Lone Star Books, Houston, Texas, 1983.)

You can still visit the site of the first oil well in Texas at nearby Oil Springs if you persevere and don't let a red mud road and dense undergrowth deter you. Sadly, Tol was never able to get financing for his Melrose Petroleum Company, so Pennsylvania became the first oil-producing state rather than Texas.

Tol's home was destined for destruction by its owner who wanted to use the wood for a barn. Captain Charles and Ann Phillips were appalled that such a historic landmark would be destroyed, so they bought the house and moved it to their property and lovingly restored it. With help from the Barret grandchildren, if Tol came home today, he would find it much as it was at his death in 1913.

Many of the Barret's original possessions are still here such as their marriage certificate, their portrait, and the accounts ledger Tol used when he was a storekeeper. Each entry tells a story of life in Texas' oldest town.

Tol's favorite colors were used, and pieces added and duplicated as closely as possible to the grandchildren's memories of their ancestor.

Tucked away in the Piney Woods of East Texas near Nacogdoches, the Tol Barret House stands as a memorial to the man who discovered Texas' first oil well.

A Barret family tradition was to ask guests to sign the front door, and the Phillips are continuing the tradition. The first name is "Bill Clements, 9-22-81," signed on the 115th anniversary of the day Tol Barret struck oil.

The yard is kept just as the Barrets did, in a "swept garden" surrounded by a pole fence. Every blade of grass was pulled out and the yard swept clean with a stick broom to keep out grass that might hide rodents and snakes. Flower beds often filled with roses were planted in geometric designs such as the Texas Star and were lined with ale bottles. The Phillips have recreated the yard, but the ale bottles have been replaced with beer bottles from the local honky tonk. However, Ann still uses a stick broom to sweep the yard.

What would the story of Texas be without its oil moguls and great oil strikes, yet it is here in the red mud of East Texas with Tol Barret that the saga began.

Samuel Bell Maxey House

The life of Samuel Bell Maxey sounds like a history of Texas during the second half of the 19th century. His adult life began on the East Coast. After rooming with Stonewall Jackson, Maxey graduated West Point and left to serve in the Mexican War where he was promoted for gallantry. He returned to his native Kentucky where for a time he practiced law with his father, became involved in politics, and married Marilda Cass Denton.

Then the great migration west began, and the family ceased to profit from their Kentucky law practice. In 1857 the Maxeys joined the march west. The

812 South Church St.
Paris 75460
214-785-5716
Hours: 10:00–5:00, Wed.–Sun.
Admission charge

The Maxey family migrated with early settlers and built their home on the threshold to the west; here they contributed greatly to Texas' development.

young law family settled in Paris, threshold to Texas, and began serving the legal needs of pioneers seeking land. In the following years, Sam Maxey practiced law and held political office until he became actively involved in the Civil War where he attained the rank of major general. With the war over, Maxey fought a two-year struggle to obtain the special presidential pardon required of high-ranked ex-Confederate officers. When the law practice again flourished, the family constructed their home on a five acre site outside of Paris.

The childless Maxeys had adopted the daughter of one of Sam's men killed at Shiloh, and with the presence of other family members, the home buzzed with social and legal activity. However, the ex-confederate officer's involvement with politics was not over. Soon Samuel, the first democratic senator to be elected from the post-war South, was off to Washington. In his absence Marilda busied herself by completing the house interior and expanding the extensive gardens. She purchased furniture, oriental carpets, and many decorative accessories during trips to Washington and St. Louis. Special items were ordered by mail from New Orleans; others came from the Babcock Furniture Co. in Paris. For the next few years this house of high Victorian Italianate style became a focal point of activities affecting legal and governmental events. Finally, after 12 years in the Senate, Maxey returned to Paris where he practiced law until his death.

The house was eventually inherited by his grandson, Samuel Bell Maxey Long, who remodeled it in 1911. Much of the refurbishing is evident upstairs where an original family bedroom suite graces one room. The first family settee and chair, with original coverings, retain their place of prominence in the dog trot area. Upstairs closets, boxes, and racks contain fashionable clothing worn by family members of all ages. Even the original wedding shoes worn by Marilda Maxey in 1853 await inspection by antique clothing connoisseurs as well as someone's beautifully preserved beaver hat.

The park superintendent enchants visitors with Civil War stories involving local and regional citizens under the command of Major General Maxey. At Christmas time the local council of garden clubs takes great pains to decorate the old mansion and offer their special version of a Victorian Yuletide.

(See color photo.)

Ezekiel Cullen House

At some date prior to 1835, Ezekiel Cullen migrated from Georgia to San Augustine, Texas, bringing with him a law degree, ten thousand dollars, a body servant, and his "true daughter of the Old South" wife. Early Texas provided ample opportunities for the ambitious Ezekiel Cullen. He practiced law as an active member of the San Augustine bar association from 1837–48; was a member of the third Congress of the Texas Republic in 1838–39, representing San Augustine in the House; was judge of the First Judicial District and associate justice of the Supreme Court of the Republic of Texas; and authored bills setting aside public lands to support education. In 1839, a master builder, Augustus Phelps, constructed the home where Judge Cullen and his family lived until 1850 when President Taylor appointed Cullen purser of the U. S. Navy and the family moved to Washington. After the Civil War, the Elisha Roberts family lived in the house, and then Grandson Hugh Roy Cullen purchased the property and commissioned its restoration in 1952; he presented it to the Ezekiel Cullen Chapter of the Daughters of the Republic of Texas who presently oversee the care and considerable use of this lovely old home.

Perhaps the outstanding architectural feature of Judge Cullen's home is the Texas Star which is centered over the double door molding. The Greek Revival style with Doric columns was used for the simple one-story house, but the garret was finished as a ballroom and extends the entire length of the house with fan-shaped windows at each end. Today, the garret ballroom is used as a museum area with a collection of historic memorabilia.

Townspeople enjoy the Cullen Home as a community house and museum, and since members of the Daughters of the Republic of Texas are responsible for overseeing its use, photos of the charter members line the entrance hall along with charter documentation. Beautiful period antiques decorate the parlor with a portrait of Ezekiel Cullen's father hanging over the mantel. Opposite the parlor the S. Seymour Thomas Memorial Room houses a collection of work by this artist and

Market at Cullen Sts.
San Augustine 75972
409-275-3610
Hours: 1:00–4:00, Mon.–Sat.
Admission charge

Judge Ezekiel Cullen occupied his home in San Augustine until he moved to Washington. Grandson Hugh Roy Cullen commissioned restoration of the house in 1952.

portrait painter, born in San Augustine and acclaimed around the world. The grounds surrounding the home are kept in excellent condition, and guides point with pride to the back patio surface of hand-made bricks from slave days.

San Augustine and Nacogdoches have long disputed which is the oldest town in Texas; each claims the honor. You might enliven your visit to either town by asking a local citizen to explain which one was really first.

(See color photo.)

Griffin Memorial House

P. O. Box 457
Tomball 77357
713-255-2148
Hours: Mar.–Dec.
2:00–5:00, Sun.
Jan.–Feb.
10:00–2:00, Thurs.
or by appointment
Admission charge

Almost hidden away at the end of a quiet, shaded street in northwest Harris County sits the Tomball Community Museum Center, home to the Griffin Memorial House. What a pleasant surprise awaits those who venture to the north end of Pine Street where among several other historic buildings of equal interest is found the quaint old home first built in 1860 by a Frenchman, Eugene Pillot. Though his family first immigrated to New York in 1832, when he was only twelve, they resettled in Texas in 1837 bringing with them valuable skills as carpenters and joiners. Eugene became one of the first builders of Harris County, putting up some of the first buildings erected in Houston. Later he turned his attention to the timber business and farming. About 1860 he built this house for his son. Its original location was near the route of the Atascosita Trail and on the stagecoach line. Sam Houston was a frequent guest of the Pillots as were any other important passengers on the stagecoach.

Though the house is Greek Revival in style, many New England influences are evident from the Pillots' years of residence there. The house is constructed entirely of pine from virgin timber and has the original entrance and hardware. Seldom were closets built in houses during this era since taxation was based on the number of rooms. The Pillot house, however, had built-in closets, which indicates the family was quite well off. The house changed owners several times before John Griffin bought it in 1920. The upstairs section of the old home became the civic center where it was used for school classes, quilting bees, square dances, and parties.

Present furnishings are true to the period of the house, but two items in the center hallway demand special attention. The first, a wooden cabinet of cubicles, is from Tomball's first post office. Then on the wall hangs a 200 year old Chinese tapestry woven in a stitch so tiny and difficult to achieve that it was said to have caused women to go blind. Supposedly, so many women lost their sight over this tedious needlecraft, the Emperor forbad its use; and it thus became known as the "forbidden stitch." In the daughters' bedroom are several Pillot family photos, and a unique silver jewelry box adorns the dresser in the parents' room. Brides and bridesmaids are allowed to dress in these two rooms when using the historic old church next door for weddings. Dating from 1860, the kitchen work table with corn meal and flour bins is a true Texas primitive. On the way out, children will particularly enjoy the collection of wind up toys dating from the 1920s.

No trip to the museum center would be complete without seeing the adjacent old Trinity Evangelical Lutheran Church with all its original furniture. Whatever you do, don't miss the delightful photographic display in the fellowship hall. The blowups of an early 19th century German wedding, hog butchering day, and other festive occasions are alone worth the trip to Tomball.

Goodman Museum

Today's visitors enter the lovely old Goodman museum under proudly hung United States, Texas, and Confederate flags and through a grand circular portico. When you visit Tyler's prize historic home, envision a by-gone era when Dr. W. J. Goodman, the surgeon for whom the museum was named, welcomed 19th-century guests who arrived wearing hats and gloves in horse-drawn carriages. Then imagine how different it was later when tattered, young Confederate soldiers passed the doctor's house on their way home from the war. Perhaps the beauty of the stately manor offered them a few moments of escape from the images of a lost cause, one they had thought would end so differently.

Once inside if you look to the left, you will sense an atmosphere more home than museum; there to greet his guests is a striking statue of Dr. William Goodman in full dress uniform. Displays of family personal possessions add to the

624 North Broadway
Tyler 75702
214-597-5304
Hours: 1:00–5:00, Mon.–Sat.
Free admission

United States, Texas, and Confederate flags wave over the Goodman Museum grand circular portico and welcome visitors to the by-gone era depicted inside.

touch of realism. Several old Victrolas, radios, eye glasses, a fiddle, and even some of the doctor's antiquated surgical instruments revive visions of their historical period.

Also enjoyable are the collection of clothing belonging to the Goodman daughter, Etta, and the grandfather clock (with wooden works) the elder Dr. Samuel Goodman brought with him from South Carolina to Texas in 1857. In addition to the family pieces willed to the city by Dr. Goodman's daughter, Mrs. J. H. Le-Grand, visitors today like the collection of antique memorabilia belonging to The Smith County Historical Society and an exhibit belonging to the Mollie Moore Davis chapter of the Daughters of the Confederacy.

Special appointments inside include six fireplaces, four down and two upstairs, and 12 inch wood base windows and doors with unusual molding trim. Mrs. Samuel Goodman bought the Empire and Victorian furnishings in New Orleans in 1860. China and porcelain were imported from England and France along with interesting odd pieces from around the world. The stunning circular staircase must have provided a dramatic entrance for Southern belles descending to greet their eager young suitors. This east Texas city has long been a favorite attraction to those who appreciate the beauty of her glorious October Rose Festival with its regal coronation ceremony and spectacular parade. On your next trip through Tyler, make a point to see the Goodman Museum and grounds, especially splendid during the floral weeks of spring, and relish a few memories of the era when the Old South gave birth to this stately old home, a rose forever in bloom.

(See color photo.)

Kell House

900 Bluff
Wichita Falls 76301
817-723-0623
Hours: 2:00–4:00, Sun.
Mon.–Sat. by arrangement
Admission charge

Two partners central to the economic and social life of the Wichita Falls community, Frank Kell and Joseph Kemp, emerged first in the milling business so vital in the 1880s. As times progressed and the community's needs changed, the partnership of Kemp and Kell met the challenge with ever-enlarging enterprises. When their grain empire stretched into 100 counties, these two industrious leaders built a series of railroads to provide needed transportation. Kell fathered the first power company, started the newspaper, founded a streetcar line, built the first modern office building, and developed a town. So powerful and inspiring were both halves of this team that the slogan for success became, "Think like Kemp; work like Kell."

This partnership was a very demanding one, but in spite of the tremendous demands of his business empire, Frank Kell neglected neither his family of wife and six children nor his community responsibilities. The Kell House became a gathering place for state and national leaders, and from here his family was encouraged to contribute where their talents were needed. During World War I, one daughter, Miss Willie May, presided over a Red Cross chapter right in the Kell House parlor, but the energetic lass was not content to stay home. Instead, she went to France and helped the Red Cross there in post-war efforts. Joseph, the only son, served his country as a soldier. Not to be outdone by her children, Mrs. Kell served too by driving the town's first electric car, always with a bouquet of fresh flowers inside, to carry shut-ins to the Presbyterian church.

Continuing to use the Kell House in its tradition of service, the Wichita County Historical Society now organizes several annual events at which people can share holiday fun. A very special July Fourth celebration enlivens the grounds around the old home on our nation's birthday. Annually, thousands of children seat themselves in the receiving hall while special "living" Christmas stories are enacted. Husbands can depend on the Kell House volunteers to sell the perfect Valentine present for their wives.

When you visit this lovely old mansion, you first enter the receiving/living room. A portrait of Mr. Kell hangs over the fireplace facing the front door. He seems to be guarding the two adjacent rooms, each furnished with pieces used by the Kell family. The redecorated, formal parlor has a resplendent French feeling with Louis XV style furniture, pale green carpet, and soft cream-colored walls. Two elegant alabaster urns adorn the mantel. Portraits of Mrs. Kell and her mother hang in the spacious dining room where these two gracious ladies entertained frequently with dinner parties. An old-fashioned kitchen connects the dining room to a cheerful, enclosed sun porch where the Kells, the only family to ever live here, enjoyed breakfasts and grew flowers.

Upstairs, evidence abounds that the majority of this household was female. Ladies' dresses are on display, and you can almost hear the buzzing of activity from the sewing room where each season a dressmaker was in residence to clothe the young women. The Kell family enjoyed a close relationship and a good sense of humor; the girls often sewed and embroidered while their father read aloud. The only son, Joseph, became his father's "right hand," and when the doctor suggested Frank Kell let his son run the business and get a hobby to preserve his weakening health, he bought a pool table. Always the dutiful wife, Mrs. Kell began playing pool with her husband; however, she always concealed this "unladylike" activity from the town folk by pulling down the shade.

The Wichita Falls County Historical Society raised the money to buy this lovely old mansion. This special group of people now continue serving the local community in the Kell tradition by opening the carefully preserved home for tours that awaken the public awareness of the role Kell House played in local and national heritage.

(See color photo.)

✦ THE GULF COAST ✦

John Jay French House

Long famous for its Spindletop gusher, Beaumont was the beginning of the gigantic oil industry in Texas. However, Beaumont was a town long before Spindletop blew in on January 10, 1901. Back in 1845 Beaumont was an up-and-coming commercial center on the Opelousas Trail connecting Louisiana to Washington-on-the-Brazos. An enterprising Yankee realized the rich potential of the new settlement, and went shopping for a new site for his business and home.

John Jay French was a seventh-generation American born in 1799 in Woodbridge, Connecticut, no mean accomplishment in 1799. French married Sally Munson of New Haven in 1819 and later moved to New York State where he established himself in merchandising and tanning.

John and Sally, as did thousands of others, decided about 1831 to make their fortune in Texas. So, in 1835, French brought his family as far as Louisiana, where he waited out Texas' revolution. He had spent a year amassing goods, but unfortunately the ship transporting most of his stock was lost in a storm. Undaunted, French arrived in Beaumont and selected 300 oak-covered acres for his home, tannery, and trading post.

The canny merchant built his wife a magnificent house, like no one in those parts had ever seen. Sally's home represented a number of firsts for Beaumont; the first house made of lumber instead of logs, the first two-story house, and the first house that was painted. But then, John Jay came from a cultured New England background and wanted the best for his family. He even brought, at great expense, an 1838 box piano to the frontier. Homes for his married children were built and the trading post soon became "French Town."

At the age of 86, John French decided the country was too civilized for him, so he and Sally moved west and lived their remaining years in Taylor County. In 1968 the historic French home became the property of the Beaumont Heritage Society, and restoration was begun.

With Raiford Stripling as resident architect, a recently added facade was peeled away and the structure reduced to its original four downstairs rooms and one huge room upstairs. The house, with its "dogtrot" hallway, is similar to numerous Greek Revival Texas homes. A common feature of these homes was a "swept yard" which was scraped of grass and packed into a hard surface. This practical feature made it easy to spot snakes and keep other unwelcome creatures from coming into the house. The ceilings still have their original blue paint that early settlers thought would repel flying insects and nesting birds.

Descendants of the French family contributed many items to enhance the authenticity of the restoration. Original pieces such as a music box, most likely from England, and the French family Bible were among the treasured donations.

As you climb the steep, narrow stairs, you find a bedroom-nursery. A crib opens on one side to fit next to the bed, a nursing rocker tips far back, and a tiny oil lamp that served as a night light sits nearby. A child's handmade leather shoes (each the same size, no left or right) wait beside a trundle bed.

French is still a well-recognized name around Beaumont. Streets, schools and a variety of local landmarks still bear the pioneer's name. Now completely surrounded by the city, French House is tucked away in a group of thick trees hidden from the modern world, retaining its historic charm.

(See color photo.)

2995 French Road
Beaumont 77706
409-898-0348
Hours: 10:00–4:00, Tues.–Sat.
1:00–4:00, Sun.
Admission charge

McFaddin-Ward House

1906 McFaddin Avenue
Beaumont 77701
409-832-1906
Hours: One-hour tours
  10:00–4:00, Tues.–Sat.
  1:00–4:00, Sun.
  Reservations requested

Texas' "Golden Age" lasted from 1895 to 1982, the same years as Mamie Mc-Faddin Ward's life, and her magnificent home is an appropriate symbol of Texas' opulent past. This Beaux Arts Colonial mansion was the product of a Beaumont architect, Henry Conrad Mauer, and was constructed in 1906 for W. C. and Di McFaddin Averill. In 1907 Averill sold the house to his brother-in-law, W. P. H. McFaddin and his wife Ida Caldwell. McFaddin, "the wealthiest man in southeast Texas," was shrewd enough to own the land underneath the Spindletop gusher, plus numerous other lucrative investments.

The imposing McFaddin-Ward House in Beaumont was the home of "the wealthiest man in southeast Texas."

The McFaddins spared no expense in furnishing their 17-room mansion, and the couple became the leaders in Beaumont society. Their only daughter, Mamie McFaddin Ward, inherited the house and carried on as Beaumont's grande dame. Before her death, Mamie established a foundation for the restoration and preservation of her historic home. Now open as a museum, the McFaddin-Ward House is as magnificent as it was in 1907. It was praised by the Texas Historical Society as "the most perfect specimen of the palatial style of architecture extant in the entire Gulf Coast region of Texas."

Colossal two-story Ionic columns dominate the entrance and one-story identical Ionic columns are on both sides of the elaborate beveled glass doors. The wide

THE GULF COAST ❧ 41

spacious porches were the setting for many fetes. Shaded by gigantic oaks grown from acorns picked up at the San Jacinto Battleground, an orchestra played lilting dances, and as many as 36 tables of guests played cards and sipped iced drinks on Texas summer evenings. Surprisingly, the porch ceiling is painted green rather than the traditional Victorian blue. Blue was usually used in the hope that birds would think the ceiling was the sky, and wouldn't nest in the intricate gingerbread trim.

Ida McFaddin did not use a decorator's expertise, but her own conservative and traditional taste to furnish her home. Today her taste would be considered anything but conservative. The opulent entry features unique metallic leather coats-of-arms medallions on the portieres, ornate woodwork and marquetry panels. Crystal lamps illuminate the massive carved newel posts and reflect the rich colors in the Persian rugs. All of the draperies in the house are exact replicas of the originals, and it boggles the mind to estimate the cost of duplication.

The jeweled showpiece of the house is the Pink Parlor, to the left of the entry. Louis XV-style furniture (American made) and rich pink Damask upholstered sofa and chairs complement the delicately hand-painted pattern of trailing vines and rosebuds on the walls and ceiling.

In a corner chest is a strange little collection of treasures. Some are rare and expensive and others as mundane as common seashells. The Victor talking machine, circa 1911, is finished in the Vernis Martin method with handpainted flowers and pastoral scenes. It is no wonder that Mamie chose this beautiful room for her marriage to Carroll E. Ward in 1919.

Brilliant cut glass and gleaming silver abound in the huge dining room with its two sideboards. Repousse silver flatware, place sets, and goblets set the formal table with its exquisite tablecloth of bobbin lace, needlepoint lace, embroidery, and cut work. Every piece gleams and sparkles in the reflection of the chandeliers dripping with crystal spires.

One of the most interesting rooms in the house is the breakfast room/conservatory with its fabulous stained glass windows and marble fountain and Art Nouveau statue. Every room in the house has its special stained glass window, but these in the conservatory are exceptional.

Bedrooms are named for the prominent color of their decor. The Pink Bedroom was redecorated in 1940 and reflects Mamie's taste in New Orleans-style ornate furniture. The Blue and Green Bedrooms represent guest rooms from the 1940–1960 period, but the Master Bedroom is Ida McFaddin's choice with a handsome four-poster bed, a New Orleans chiffonier, and a "Napoleon" desk.

Of course, restoration of this wonderful mansion was a monumental task. Amazingly, the wiring and plumbing met the city codes and did not have to be replaced, but all light fixtures had to be rewired. Cleaning was done by professional conservators who analyzed, finished, and restored the painted walls and ceilings and determined cleaning methods. The grounds were completely relandscaped and a rose garden was reestablished.

Mamie McFaddin Ward was a beloved philanthropist and volunteered many hours to her community and made many major gifts to Beaumont's churches and schools. However, none of her gifts can compare with the magnificent home she has left behind to her town and to Texas.

(See color photo.)

Egypt Plantation

10 miles north of Wharton on FM 102

Contact: Anita Northington
P. O. Box 277
Egypt 77436
409-677-3562
Hours: Tours by reservation only
Admission charge

The story of Egypt, Texas, is somewhat along the lines of the biblical story of Jacob who was sold into slavery in Egypt by his jealous brothers. But Jacob, with his gift for dream interpretation, was able to predict a coming famine, enabling Egypt to be the only nation prepared for it. All the surrounding people, including Jacob's brothers, were forced to come to Egypt to buy grain. In 1827 there was a terrible drought in Wharton County and rain fell on only one small portion, John C. Clark's grant. The starving colonists came to Clark for grain and called it "going down into Egypt for corn." The name stuck, and a small settlement called Egypt began.

Stephen and Jemima Heard came to Texas from Tennessee with Austin's second colony in the late 1820s and were given their land grants in 1830. Their eldest son, William Jones Elliott Heard, struck out on his own and purchased about 2,000 acres in the Egypt settlement in the early 1830s and married the lovely America Morton.

Commissioned a captain, Heard answered the call to arms in 1836 and joined General Sam Houston in Gonzales and commanded Company F, which was made up of men from Egypt. In 1840 he campaigned against the Indians, and again in 1842, Captain Heard was called to fight for Texas against the Woll invasion of San Antonio.

Heard began construction in 1847 of a double dog-trot Georgian house on the highest point of his Egypt land. Built by his slaves using brick made from the banks of Caney Creek, his home was completed in 1849. It was inherited by Heard's daughter and son-in-law, Elizabeth and Menton Northington. Their descendants have lived in the house until the present day, and it is considered one of the finest and oldest Anglo homes in Texas.

Egypt Plantation quickly became the social center of the community, and one of the first Methodist Church services in Texas was conducted in its parlor. Stories abound of hunting parties chasing bear and deer on Egypt land.

Today there is little left of this historic bit of Texas, but Egypt Plantation House is almost the way Captain Heard and America left it. Of course, modern conveniences have been added as well as a large "keeping room," or living room. Everywhere you look are marvelous antiques, and each one has a special story. In the long bar are cases of papers, stamps, Confederate bonds and even a copy of the land grant signed by Stephen F. Austin.

In the original part of the house, the gleaming floors are constructed of wood from East Texas, and oriental rugs add to their beauty. A huge wooden chest in the dog trot is now packed with ancient quilts, but during 1836 it was packed with the family treasures and buried when Santa Anna's army threatened the plantation.

Many of the family heirlooms fill the house. Aunt Clarissa's fragile dresses and tiny shoes are here, as is a dresser with a secret drawer and a rare sofa pillow with a Frederick Remington painting on its cover and Remington's signature beneath it. Even a ghost inhabits a bedroom, that of a Confederate soldier with an amputated leg.

In the rear of the house is a small museum filled with all sorts of Civil War and pioneer artifacts that was orginally the old Egypt Santa Fe Railroad depot built in 1900.

So, when you "go down to Egypt land," your bounty won't be corn but a wonderful lesson in Texas history.

(See color photo.)

Fulton Mansion (Oakhurst)

Before the turn of the century, the southern part of the Texas coast was famous for its ranches, and one of the great cattle barons was a Yankee engineer from Baltimore. George Fulton, an extremely intelligent man far ahead of his time, first came to Texas in 1837.

Finding Texas to his liking, Fulton stayed and formed a partnership with Henry Smith, former provisional governor of Texas. It wasn't long before the brilliant Yankee fell in love with his partner's oldest daughter, Harriet, and in 1840 George formed a tie with Texas that would last his lifetime.

After their marriage the Fultons moved to Baltimore. George had a successful career as an engineer and even worked with John A. Roebling, designer of the Brooklyn Bridge. But, Texas was to be the final home for the Fultons. Harriet's father died, and she inherited most of his extensive estate, so the Fultons returned to Harriet's home in 1868.

For a couple with the Fulton's wealth and social standing, only a magnificent mansion would be appropriate, so in 1877 the Fultons moved into the specially built Oakhurst, one of the most modern and innovative houses in Texas, a showcase of Victorian splendor. A carbide gas plant provided lighting, and a large cistern in the tower gravity-fed water to the bathrooms. Each of the three floors had a bathroom with a tile floor, flush toilet, marble lavatory, and a copper bathtub with *hot* and cold running water.

Central heat was supplied by a large cast iron furnace that blew hot air through ducts to every room. Hot air was also piped into the laundry room were clothes were hung to dry, and false fireplaces concealed heating ducts. What exquisite luxury for those damp cold Texas coast winters.

George prospered in Texas in the cattle business, and on March 12, 1890, the Fultons celebrated their fiftieth wedding anniversary with a splendid golden wedding soiree at their magnificent mansion. More than 500 invitations were sent, and a special train brought guests from San Antonio. A brief three years later, Oakhurst was dark and deserted. George had died, and Harriet could not bear her home without him. Oakhurst was sold to Mr. and Mrs. J. W. Davidson.

The Davidsons lived in Oakhurst for many years, but by 1938 hard times forced them to live on the 25-cent admission charged to visitors. For a while a restaurant and then a hotel struggled for survival in the house, but by 1976 the battered old mansion was falling into ruin in the middle of an ugly trailer park.

Fortunately for Texas, Texas Parks and Wildlife came to the rescue and purchased George and Harriet's home. Today, the Fulton Mansion is one of Texas' outstanding restorations and tourist attractions.

The grounds may not be as beautiful as Harriet kept them, but her conservatory that gave her so much pleasure is filled with plants she loved. The entry way

Fulton
Contact: Park Superintendent,
* Fulton Mansion*
* P. O. Box 1859*
* Fulton, Texas 78358*
* 512-729-0386*
Hours: 9:00–12:00, 1:00–4:00,
* Wed.–Sun.*

Admission charge

still has its lovely Minton tile floor and original chandelier. The Davidsons had removed the fixture, but their descendants returned it, and its plaster medallion was put together piece by piece on the ceiling like a jigsaw puzzle. Amazingly, all of the original mirrors are still intact and survived fierce Gulf Coast storms without cracking.

Note that the carpets are sewn in strips, as this was how Victorian carpet was installed. During the dusty Texas summers rugs were rolled up and stored, and the furniture was shrouded in dust covers. Harriet was a perfect housekeeper and had seven servants to keep her home spotless.

On the second floor is Harriet's sewing room and ladies' parlor. She loved to work Battenberg lace, and the unusual sewing kit she may have used is called a "housewife." In the bedrooms note the strange pockets hanging on the walls next to the beds. These were for bedroom slippers to keep them off of cold floors.

The third floor is not open for tours, but there is a tower room called the "Growlery" where George retired to watch his ships or perhaps to just let off steam.

Fulton's magnificent French Second Empire-style house with its mansard roof was built of the finest materials by master craftsmen and reflects Fulton's superior talents as a designer. Because of his meticulous planning, George Fulton's mansion has survived hurricanes, storms, and the worst threat of all—progress. It is as though the years never passed, and Oakhurst is once again the showcase of the Gulf Coast.

Ashton Villa

2328 Broadway
Galveston
Contact: Ashton Villa
P. O. Box 1616
Galveston 77553
409-762-3933
Hours: 10:00–4:00, Mon.–Fri.
12:00–5:00, Sat.–Sun.
Admission charge

Since 1859 Ashton Villa has serenely withstood the onslaughts of both man and nature—the Civil War, the 1900 Storm, Hurricanes Carla and Alicia, and even the very real threat of demolition.

This grand Italianate mansion was built by James Moreau Brown, Galveston's wealthy merchant and entrepreneur, for his lively family and as a setting for their lavish entertaining. Brown designed his regal mansion himself and named it in honor of Isaac Ashton, a Revolutionary forebear of his wife. This was the first brick house in Galveston, and Brown owned the brick yard. From the mansion's balcony, the Emancipation Proclamation was read on June 16.

After the 1900 Great Storm, Galveston raised the level of the island, and the fill covered in Ashton Villa's basement. Note the short iron fence around the house. Before the fill, this fence was over six feet tall.

The Villa remained in the Brown family until the 1920s when the El Mina Shrine Temple purchased it. In 1971, the Shriners announced plans to demolish the building, and a horrified Galveston Historical Foundation and City of Galveston bought the property. The next three years were devoted to restoring Ashton Villa to its original opulence, and the restoration was placed under the direction of architect Raiford Stripling.

Ashton Villa has serenely withstood the onslaughts of both man and nature—even Galveston's devastating 1900 storm did not mar its beauty.

Photographs were available and of immense help in furnishing the mansion. Some original pieces are still where they were placed by the Browns, and other original furnishings are finding their way back to the house. Using the photographs as a guide, many authentic Victorian antiques have been added to complete the beautiful rooms.

In the Gold Room with its very formal rococo furniture, the two pier mirrors and gold leaf cornices are all original. Note the water mark on the mirrors where the rooms were flooded. The exquisite staircase is in prime condition, and the handrail consists of only two pieces of wood handcarved from a single block. When the Brown's youngest daughter, Matilda, married, the staircase was painted white to match her dress.

Brown did not like wallpaper, so the walls were painted. And he preferred wall-to-wall carpeting instead of the usual oriental rugs found in most Victorian homes. The oldest Brown daughter, Bettie, was an artist, and much of the wall space was hung with her works, none of which were ever sold. Bettie never married and turned down many proposals, and then shocked Galveston by going off *alone* on cruises and studying art in Europe. This flamboyant lady's paintings of *nude* angels were considered very risque for Galveston society. On the third floor of the Villa was the ballroom and Miss Bettie's studio. Her bedroom on the second floor is furnished with her original furniture, including her bed linens initialed "B."

In Matilda's room the furniture is not original. Matilda divorced and returned home with her three children. The Brown girls were certainly not your typical Victorian ladies.

Brown included total luxury in his home. *Every* room had a closet and a gas fireplace, and the house had running water with a cistern in the attic. The walls of the Villa are three bricks deep, and the windows facing the beach are triple hung. As expected, the Browns had the first telephone in Galveston.

Here at Ashton Villa the romance and gaiety of Victorian Galveston lingers on. In settings virtually unchanged since the 19th century, the past is yours to experience.

(See color photo.)

Bishop's Palace

1402 Broadway
Galveston 77550
409-762-2475
Hours: 10:00–5:00 daily, 12:00–5:00,
Sun.,
May 31 to Labor Day
Winter tours: 12:00–4:00
Closed Tuesday
Admission charge

Of all the opulent and grandiose historic homes in Texas, none can match the splendor of the Bishop's Palace, but before it became a palace, this magnificent mansion was a castle.

In the 1880s Galveston was "Queen of the Gulf" and drew fortune hunters of all persuasions, including one impecunious young man named Walter E. Gresham. This former Confederate colonel was present at the sad surrender at Appomattox. He arrived in Galveston poor, but ambitious, and with a law degree from the University of Virginia. By 1886 Gresham was one of the wealthiest men in Texas, and he was determined to build the most elaborate house in his adopted state. It took seven years, from 1886 to 1893, to build his home, and the people of Galveston called it "Walter Gresham's Castle." Gresham did live like a king indeed, and he and his wife, 9 children, and 13 servants reigned over the castle for 27 years.

Gresham was fortunate to secure the services of Nicholas J. Clayton, the designer of many fine homes and buildings in Galveston, and the late 19th century in Galveston became known as the "Clayton Era."

For the house Gresham and Clayton had in mind, ships brought in native Texas granite, limestone, and sandstone. Numidian marble came from Italy, onyx and silver from Mexico, crystal chandeliers from Venice, damask from England, and exotic woods from forests around the world. The incredible handcarved oak staircase that dominates the first floor was floated down the Mississippi from Cincinnati. It took 66 craftsmen as long to carve the staircase as it did Gresham to build his castle.

By today's prices Gresham got a real bargain for his 25-room, 4-story home. He estimated the cost to be an unheard-of $250,000 (others believed it closer to $350,000).

The style of the castle ranges from French Renaissance to Italian Romanesque with Galveston ironwork porches. Towers are topped with Medieval tiled cones, and chimneys, both real and false, give the impression of a cluster of large houses.

The granite steps to the entry are flanked by fierce gargoyles, and over the entrance is the stone face of Gresham's youngest daughter, Beulah. Inside is the overwhelming beauty of three stained and jeweled glass windows. The stained glass window depicting Saint Theresa replaces one of jeweled glass that was blown out in a hurricane.

Equally as gorgeous as the windows are the 14 wood and coal fireplaces. No two are alike, and the one decorated with silver and onyx won a prize at the New Orleans Exposition of 1886. The mahogany and marble fireplace in the front parlor won first prize at the Philadelphia World's Fair in 1876.

Gresham's Castle became the Bishop's Palace in 1923 when it became the residence of Bishop Christopher E. Byrne of the Catholic Diocese of Galveston until his death in 1950. He often called the house "my palace in the sky." One of the second-floor bedrooms was converted into an exquisite chapel with lovely stained glass windows and religious paintings, and it is maintained as the bishop left it.

No matter how often you tour the Bishop's Palace, you are bound to see something special every time. It was truly built to last through eternity with its 23-inch thick, steel-reinforced stone walls. After the Great Storm of 1900 the Greshams opened their house to hundreds of refugees, for the house was completely undamaged.

Everywhere are touches of luxury. As a special convenience for the long-haired Gresham ladies, the bathroom had three water lines—one for hot, one for cold, and one for *rainwater*. Cooking was done in the basement on 17 stoves, and the house was wired for electricity and even indirect lights before electricity was available to private homes.

The American Institute of Architects has recognized the Bishop's Palace as one of the 100 outstanding structures built during the first 100 years of that group's activity. In addition, it is on a list of 15 buildings included in the Archives of the Library of Congress as representative of early American architecture. The Bishop's Palace is the only building in the country on both lists.

The Catholic Diocese of Houston and Galveston still maintains the home, and many future generations will share the beauty and magnificence of the "Castle" and the "Palace."

Sam Williams Home

Sam Houston, Davy Crockett, William B. Travis—all of those names are known to every Texan, but one of the real heroes of Texas rarely rates a mention in the history books. Yet, without Sam Williams, there may not have been a Republic of Texas. (See *Unsung Heroes of Texas*, Lone Star Books, Houston, Texas, 1986.)

Sam came to Texas in 1822, and during those early years he served as Stephen F. Austin's secretary and land officer. Because of Williams' meticulous attention to detail with the colonists' land titles, he set the basis for recording deeds today.

When the revolution began, Williams was in partnership with Thomas McKinney. Not only did they raise money for Texas, they personally loaned the Republic $100,000, a very hefty sum in 1835. (An ungrateful Texas repaid only $40,000.) It was also Sam Williams who arranged to acquire the six small ships of the Texas Navy.

3601 Avenue P
Galveston 77550
Contact: Galveston Historical
Foundation
2016 The Strand
Galveston 77550
409-765-7834
Hours: 12:00–4:00, daily
Admission charge

This home in Galveston was the residence of Sam Williams, who not only was "the financier of the Texas Revolution," but also "the father of Texas banking."

In 1836 McKinney and Williams moved to Galveston and invested in shipping, real estate, and banking. In fact, Williams became "the father of Texas banking." Texans had a deep mistrust of banks, and Williams was persecuted by anti-banking factions. Sam experienced more bitterness over this project than any other service he rendered to Texas.

When he died in 1858, his doctor diagnosed his death as, "a giving way mentally and physically."

In 1839, Sam built his beloved wife, Sarah, and their children a fine house high on brick piers to protect it from flooding. The Williams House was probably one of Texas' first prefabricated homes. Framed in Maine, the members were numbered and shipped to the present site where a Galveston carpenter reassembled them. It was furnished in the latest style with damask curtains, elegant furniture, and a handsome grand piano with mother-of-pearl keys. The story goes that the piano was thrown overboard from a ship that ran aground near Galveston.

The house was sold to the Lucher family who inhabited it nearly 100 years, but by 1955 Sarah's home was a haunted house for neighborhood children. The Galveston Historical Foundation bought a dilapidated wreck, and it took until 1984 to finance and accomplish the restoration.

Your tour begins with a brief slide show of vintage illustrations, and actors portray Sam, his family, and the McKinneys. In the rooms you listen to recorded conversations of daily life in the house as Sam and McKinney argue about banking problems, and little Sam and his father build kites.

The house is furnished much as it was in 1854 with pieces selected on the basis of Sam's bills and letters in the Williams Collection of Galveston's Rosenberg Library. The reclining chair actually rested Sam's weary bones, and the silver eyeglass case was a gift from Sam Houston.

The financial genius becomes a real living person in his home, and in one recording he says, "So much time has passed. I turned my head for a moment, and they were all grown . . . can you tell me where the years have gone?" The years have gone, but at last Sam Williams is given his recognition as one of the great Texas heroes, thanks to the Galveston Historical Foundation.

(See color photo.)

Bayou Bend

The story of the restoration of historic homes in Texas almost begins and ends with the state's greatest philanthropist, Miss Ima Hogg. The only daughter of Sarah Ann and James Stephen Hogg, Texas' first native born governor, was born on July 10, 1882, in Mineola. She was christened Ima for the heroine of a long epic poem by her uncle Thomas Elisha Hogg. In spite of her name, this great lady gave so much of her time and fortune to Texas that she will always be loved and remembered as "Miss Ima."

No. 1 Westcott
Houston
713-529-8773
Hours: 10:00–2:45, Tues.–Fri.
10:00–11:45, Sat.
Admission charge. Minimum age 14.

Miss Ima's list of accomplishments and donations reads on and on. In 1913 she organized Houston's first symphony concert and thus began her lifelong dedication to the symphony and Houston's Museum of Fine Arts.

Miss Ima's enthusiasm, imagination, and strength of will reached into all facets of Texas history. She donated the beautiful restoration of her Varner-Hogg Plantation to the state, she gave the unique farmstead of Winedale to the University of Texas, and she helped furnish the Governor's Mansion with priceless antiques. In 1955 she gave her 15-acre estate, Bayou Bend, and 750,000 shares of stock for maintenance, to the Houston Museum of Fine Arts.

Honor upon honor was bestowed on Miss Ima, including ones from Presidents Eisenhower and Kennedy. In 1972, more than 300 special friends celebrated the Great Lady of Texas' 90th birthday at Winedale. Miss Ima died at age 93 and her passing was a great and irreplaceable loss to Texas. Miss Ima's funeral was held at her beautiful Bayou Bend, and she was buried at Oakwood Cemetery in Austin.

Buffalo Bayou twists and turns its way through Houston's wealthy homes, its slums, and its urban highrises. On a bend in this famous bayou is located Miss Ima's fabled Bayou Bend home with its museum collection of antiques. The house was designed by the architect John Staub for Miss Ima, and her brothers, Mr. Will and Mr. Mike Hogg, and built in the Spanish Colonial style during the years 1927-1928. The Hoggs wanted a house that "looked well on 14 acres." It does not just look well; Bayou Bend is magnificent.

You begin your tour in the foyer with the 1971 painting of Miss Ima by Robert Joy. There are no ropes around the collection, but you must stay within the guidelines pointed out by the docents. Photographs are not allowed, and you must also check your purses before starting the tour.

In the first small parlor the furniture was crafted by John Henry Belter, a superior cabinetmaker who immigrated from Germany. All of the furniture in the Philadelphia Hall was of the Chippendale Period and made in Philadelphia between 1760 and 1790. The drawing room is also furnished in the Chippendale period and contains the third finest collection in the United States. An original oil, a self-portrait by Charles Wilson Peal is dated 1788, and one of 17 additional Washington portraits by Gilbert Stuart dated 1796 hang from the walls of this perfectly appointed room.

The Pine Room, so called for its pine paneling, was Miss Ima's favorite room and the one where she put her Christmas tree. The furniture is William and Mary, dated about 1700.

The Newport Room exhibits Miss Ima's collection of silver and the Texian Room her campaign ware dishes. Made especially in England during the Mexican War, part of the campaign ware collection is also on display at the Varner-Hogg Plantation. The portrait in the Texian Room is of Miss Ima's grandfather who was a general in the Civil War. From the Texian Room is a great view of the formal English garden.

Furnishings in the Federal Parlor date from 1790 to 1810 and eagles fly everywhere—on the George Washington clock made in France, on the chests, and even the intricate sconces. In the Queen Anne Bedroom note the most unusual Japanese chest. It was made in Boston and only three are in existence. You will also enjoy the many mementoes and photographs from Miss Ima's life.

A few more wonderful rooms with incredible antiques are open for viewing, and the tour lasts about an hour and a half. Even then, as thorough as the docents' descriptions are, you are ready to go back and see it all again, for it is very difficult to absorb the scope of Miss Ima's fabulous acquisitions in one brief visit.

Sam Houston Park

1100 Bagby
Houston 77002
713-759-9217
Hours: 10:00–4:00, Mon.-Sat.
1:00–5:00, Sun.
Admission charge

Surrounded by Houston's gleaming towers of glass and steel exists a real anachronism among these modern skyscrapers—Sam Houston Park. Here you can return to the colorful past of Harris County among a collection of 6 historic homes, an 1891 Lutheran Church, and a reconstruction of Houston's first business buildings, the Long Row.

Kellum-Noble House

The handsome Greek Revival Kellum-Noble House is the oldest surviving brick house in Houston. Constructed in 1847 by Nathaniel Kellum, it is the only building in the park on its original site. Kellum became Houston's first contractor, and his house reflects his affluence.

The Kellum-Noble House is the oldest surviving brick home in Houston. This handsome Greek Revival-style home once housed one of Houston's first schools.

Wonderful antiques have been collected to enhance all of the structures in the park, but here at the Kellum-Noble House the sofa belonged to Vernal Lea, Sam Houston's brother-in-law. The lady in the portrait reading the Bible is Nancy Lea, Sam's mother-in-law, and the sideboard was Sam's.

When the Nobles acquired the house in the 1850s, Mrs. Zerviah M. Noble conducted one of Houston's first schools. Even today one of the rooms is a charming schoolroom, and third and fourth grade students are welcome to "attend class" here as they did so many years ago.

Nichols-Rice-Cherry House

Wander on down the walk to the handsome Nichols-Rice-Cherry House. This Greek Revival home was built about 1850 by Ebeneezer B. Nichols. Between 1856 and 1873 it was owned by William Marsh Rice, the famous financier. In 1897 the house was saved from demolition and moved from its original site by Mrs. E. Richardson Cherry.

You are immediately overwhelmed with the gorgeous woodwork, but close examination reveals it is common pine painted to resemble fine wood, a process called graining. The detached kitchen is so well equipped for the era that during the Christmas Candlelight Tour, docents prepare traditional holiday fare just the way Rice's servants did in those bygone days.

The Nichols-Rice-Cherry house was once owned by William Marsh Rice, the famous financier.

San Felipe Cottage

This simple, but charming six-room cottage derived its Spanish name from its location on Houston's old San Felipe Road. Actually, this 1868 house is an excellent example of an early German-Texan home. Lovely wallpaper, a massive sleigh bed of bleached mahogany, and lattice porch attest to the affluence of the family. The house has even been signed and dated by the contractor so many years ago.

This charming six-room cottage is an example of an early German-Texas home.

Pillot House

No doubt one of the most charming houses in the Sam Houston Park collection is the Eugene Pillot House. This 1868 home is a classic example of mid-Victorian elegance. Beautiful leaded glass doors open into a hall decorated with ornate wallpaper, an oriental rug, and heavy furniture so dear to the Victorian heart. In the formal parlor heavy draperies cover lace-curtained windows, and everywhere is lots of fringe and tassels.

One of the bedrooms contains a collection of lovely antique dolls that look as though the Pillot girls had just finished dressing them. Another bedroom displays a marvelous quilt made of ribbons from long-ago political conventions, as well as buttons and other convention memorabilia.

The Pillot House was innovative for its time, and it is believed to have had the very first attached kitchen in Houston. Amazingly, the family occupied this modest house until 1964, even though the Pillot family amassed a fortune in the grocery business.

The 1868 Pillot house with its beautiful leaded glass doors is a classic example of mid-Victorian elegance.

The Old Place

This cabin is the oldest structure in Harris County. It was probably built by John R. Williams, an Austin colonist, about 1824. The roughly hewn cedar logs forming the frame were incorporated by later owners into a much larger house, once known as the Joseph Davis Plantation House.

(See color photo.)

Heaven on Earth

Louisiana at Third St.
Missouri City 77459
713-499-1840
Hours: Week days only
By reservation
Admission charge

If you want a glimpse of one couple's interpretation of a celestial place, all you have to do is turn south at the 1600 block of South Main (Hwy 90A) in Missouri City and make your way to the corner of Louisiana and Third Streets. There, almost hidden among ancient live oak trees, is the enormous southern colonial plantation home Mrs. Susan Douglas Reed calls "Heaven on Earth." The arbor-like grounds, gazebo, pool, chauffeur driven limousines and 50 room mansion perhaps would more aptly be imagined as Scarlet O'Hara's Tara had she lived in the late 20th century. The exterior takes your breath away, but the unique features of its interior will make you determined to return again with friends to share this very untypical home.

The original section of the home was built in 1906 by a family with 13 children. The structure was in bad need of repair when the late J. Herbert Douglas, renowned River Oaks decorator, purchased it for his second bride who christened her new home with its celestial name. Mr. and Mrs. Douglas immediately set out to restore the house; the unique difference is that though authenticity has been preserved, a decorator's touch has been added, and that has made all the difference. Visitors first enter the parlor adorned with a striking portrait of the Douglasses and then enjoy the unique features of the study and its 1850 English banker's desk with heating bricks. Whether nature calls or not, don't miss the unique guest bath with its wood and cane potty chair. As you continue through the dining room, an enthralling leaded glass enclosed cabinet sits atop the dining room fireplace of marble and wood. Then Susan Douglas Reed's courageous taste comes into view in the almost totally red "Strawberry Morning Room."

Though the historical section of the house is worthy of touring, the unique composition of the remaining 50 + rooms tantalize even more the ardent student of antiquity. Mr. Douglas, being a superior decorator, never stopped his search for and acquisition of unusual antiques. The windows and doors of the saloon, or serving room, were purchased during the demolition of an old church and school, but a full size antique sleigh highlights the entire room. The organ came from Round Top, Texas. A step down takes you into a red and black ballroom built for the '76 Bicentennial ball on the occasion of Ronald Reagan's visit. Unfortunately, the weather did not permit his plane to land; the Reagans missed a night of lodging in a spacious loft bedroom designed and furnished especially for them. The doors, windows, and staircase used were taken from the old Hobby home on South Main, and a one-of-a-kind serving cart was originally part of a chariot from Sicily. Several other rooms follow, all red—Mrs. Douglas's favorite color, and then you enter the Green Room dominated by a 20 foot by 10 foot burled walnut cabinet, surely one of the largest pieces of furniture in existence. Nearby are two sections of the round leather-topped table used by Winston Churchill at the Swiss Embassy during World War II.

On weekends Heaven on Earth becomes the venue for weddings of all sizes. Though many rooms of the home are used for a variety of purposes on these occasions, one of the most spectacular is the Grand Hall where many of the marriage ceremonies are conducted. The beautiful old staircase from which brides now descend into the Grand Hall came from the Incarnate Word Academy. For couples who wish a smaller nuptial affair, the mini-chapel is appropriate with all antique furnishings from a church in England.

Bus tours are available for larger groups and by reservation a very "Southern" lunch can be served featuring "Heavenly Tea" and "Angel in the Cloud Cake" by Lilly, the family cook for 35 years. You will be happy you allowed at least a half day to enjoy Heaven on Earth and its quaint surroundings only a few minutes' ride out of Houston.

W. H. Stark House

If you ever wanted to know how the Victorian Era millionaires spent their money, just visit the Stark House in Orange. Completed in 1894, the mansion is built of longleaf yellow pine, and its gables, galleries, distinctive windowed turret, and fish-scale shingles present one of Texas' finest examples of Queen Anne and Eastlake Victorian architecture.

William H. Stark was one of the outstanding financial and industrial leaders of Texas in lumber, oil, rice, insurance, and banking. He married Miriam A. Lutcher, the daughter of a prominent Orange lumberman, and the Starks had one surviving son, Lutcher. All three of the Starks were avid collectors, and they could easily afford to indulge in their various hobbies.

When you enter through the carriage house for the tour, be sure to go upstairs and gasp at just a sample of Miriam's collectibles. Cases of exquisite cut glass, mostly from the "Brilliant Period," are on display as are Staffordshire animals and figures. Intricate and lovely pieces of cloisonne dominate another case, while elegant salt cellars, perfume bottles, pitchers, and Toby Jugs fill other cases. Wonderful boxes, rare porcelain figurines, and Westward Ho pressed glass are also part of the beautiful bibelots Miriam Stark loved.

Restoration of the Stark House took place between 1971 and 1981, and the results are absolutely breathtaking. A 1921 inventory of the house and furnishings was used to make every room perfect. Only the wall fabric and drapes had to be replaced, and many of the lace curtains are original. A new roof was a necessity, and the original roofing company was still in business in New Orleans and duplicated it exactly.

Front doors of hand-beveled French cut glass open into a wide entry hall graced with Meissen figurines and two unique key-hole stained glass windows. The paneling is of a rare longleaf yellow pine no longer grown, but it was in excellent condition. Throughout the entire 15 rooms are 82 antique Oriental carpets, which are taken up each summer and replaced with hooked rugs.

Each room is a showcase of Victorian wealth. The music room was Mrs. Stark's private domain with its silk-covered walls and panoply of cupids. Cupids are everywhere, even in the lace curtains, and they float lovingly around the 1900 Steinway. A cupid clock, cupid sconces, a Dresden cupid, a bronze cupid, and even a Serves urn with a cupid adorning its artistic design enhances this beautiful room.

610 Main
Orange 77630
409-883-8871
Hours: 10:00–3:30, Tues.–Sat.
Admission limited to adults and
*   children age 14 or older*
Reservations requested

The massive dining room seats 24 guests, and an excellent copy of Raphael's *Madonna and Child* hangs over the fireplace. This was Miriam's favorite painting. Huge cabinets in the pantry contain some of the Stark's three sets of dishes. Indian Tree pattern was used for formal parties and the second best china was Minton. The "everyday" china was Lennox banded in gold. Each set contains 390 pieces. Miriam certainly knew how to entertain.

W. H.'s favorite room was the masculine breakfast room with its oriental furnishings and red damask walls. Overwhelming the room is an intricately carved desk where W. H. conducted business when he wasn't in his downtown office.

The master bedroom is decorated with the furniture Miriam had as a young girl, and the guest room has all Eastlake furniture with a very rare and fine 100-percent silk oriental carpet. All of the bedrooms had a closet, which was most unusual, since closets were taxed as rooms. Many rich mansions were without closets, but not the Stark House. No luxury was overlooked.

Lutcher's room was redecorated when he went to college, and he had the distinction of being the first student at the University of Texas to have a car. Of course he took his servant as well. U. T. was also the recipient of the Stark rare book and first edition collection.

On the third floor is Miriam's dressing room and giant walk-in closet. Some of the multitude of drawers are open with her fan collection on view. The tower room was for dances, and now is decorated with numerous Napoleon pieces. Napoleon and Josephine adorn two Serves urns, and there is even a signed and numbered death mask of Napoleon.

After marveling at the magnificence of the Stark House, go over to the Stark Museum. Lutcher Stark preferred craftsmen from the American West, and he has left behind one of the finest museums of western art in the southwest. (See *Traveling Texas Borders*, Lone Star Books, Houston, 1983.)

Pompeiian Villa

1953 Lakeshore Drive
Port Arthur 77640
409-983-5977
Hours: 9:00–4:00, Mon.–Fri.
Admission charge

It is not too surprising when millionaires choose to build their home and symbol of their wealth in the style of an English manor house or even a French chateau, but Isaac Ellwood, the barbed wire king, opted for building a Roman villa in (of all places) Port Arthur.

In 1895 railroad magnate Arthur E. Stillwell founded Port Arthur, his "Dream City," as the southern terminus of his Kansas City, Pittsburgh and Gulf Railroad. After Spindletop blew in only eleven miles away, Stillwell's fortune attracted three other tycoons: John "Bet a Million" Gates, Isaac Ellwood, and James Hopkins of the Diamond Match Company. The three entrepreneurs purchased a tract of land as a site for three adjoining "winter cottages" on Lake Sabine.

Gates chose to build a colonial mansion, while Ellwood preferred to construct an unusual ten-room 79 A.D. Pompeiian Villa. Each home cost $50,000. Ellwood even budgeted the exhorbitant sum of $500,000 for a formal Roman garden similar to those of Pompeii before Mount Vesuvius wreaked its havoc, but the landscaping never materialized.

Shortly after the Villa's completion, Ellwood sold it to James Hopkins, but Mrs. Hopkins took one look at Port Arthur's mud and mosquitoes and refused to even step inside the Villa and returned home. Hopkins tried leasing the Villa, but when a land developer, George M. Craig, offered him 10 percent of his stock in a newly formed oil company in trade, Hopkins took it. Craig acquired a unique home, and Hopkins made a fortune. The new company turned out to be Texaco, and if Craig had kept his stock it would be worth about $3 billion today. So, Port Arthurians call their landmark, the "$3 billion Villa."

The next owners were Captain and Mrs. Arne Pedersen. When the Pedersens died in 1969 the house stood vacant four years. Finally, the Pedersen's niece put it on the market for $60,000, but with no takers the price dropped to $30,000. Since the Gates' mansion had been torn down, the Villa was the last vestige of those great oil boom days, and it seemed destined for the same fate as the Gates' mansion.

Finally, Mrs. William F. Fredeman, president of the Port Arthur Historical Society, convinced the seller to drop the price to $25,000 with a 6-month option. Mrs. Fredeman convinced 25 Port Arthurians, including her husband, to contribute $1,000 each, and the Villa was saved.

As you tour the Villa now, you can hardly believe so many years have passed since Ellwood completed his mansion. A local interior designer, the late Charles Martin, donated his expertise, even traveling to the ruins of Pompeii to ensure the authenticity of the colors of cerulean blue, bright red, grey, almond, green and apricot, and the exterior became a Pompeiian shade of deep pink.

Doric columns support the portico, and each window framing is slightly wider at the bottom than at the top and forms a large Roman "A." The three-sided courtyard, or peristyle, focuses on a Romanesque fountain, "Boy With A Crab," and each of the ten major rooms has its own door onto the peristyle.

Ellwood planned to furnish his summer home with antiques, so accordingly, the furnishings concentrate on styles of the turn of the century, and include a mirror authenticated as circa 1760. Many of Port Arthur's concerned citizens donated fine antiques, and former Governor Allan Shivers gave the beautiful crystal chandelier in the living room.

A Louis XI parlor set adorns the salon, and the highly ornate French diamond dust mirror is circa 18th century. One really smashing piece in the salon is the gorgeous Art Nouveau Baccarat chandelier.

The massive dining room table and chairs were made possible by a donation from the Moody Foundation, and on the floor is a rare French Savannerie rug. The impressive gentleman in the portrait is none other than "Bet-A-Million" Gates with his constant companion, "Blondie," a Boston bull terrier.

Even though most of the fine antiques and accessories were gifts, all fit together as though designed just for Pompeiian Villa. Port Arthur deserves an overwhelming vote of thanks for preserving this truly unique reminder of Port Arthur's days of splendor.

(See color photo.)

Varner-Hogg Mansion

Two miles from West Columbia on
FM 2852 off Texas 35.
Contact: Park Superintendent
Box 696
West Columbia 77486
409-345-4656
Hours: 10:00–11:00 and 1:00–4:30,
Tues–Thurs.–Fri.–Sat.
Admission charge

The story of the Varner-Hogg Plantation and Mansion begins early in Texas history, in fact with the original 300 colonists to arrive with Stephen F. Austin. The 19th "league and a labor of land" or 4,605 acres went to a trader named Martin Varner. Varner built a two-room cabin and gained the distinction of producing the first rum ever distilled in Texas. (See *Traveling Texas Borders*, Lone Star Books, Houston, 1983.)

Varner sold the land to Columbus Patton in 1834, and it remained the "Patton House" for many years. Interestingly, Columbus's older brother, William, was aide-de-campe to Sam Houston, and for a short time Santa Anna was a prisoner on the plantation.

In 1901, former governor James S. Hogg bought the property. Before his death in 1906, he was convinced oil was on his land and even drilled several dry wells. It's a shame Hogg could not have seen his plantation in 1920, for an old photograph shows the house entirely obscured by oil derricks.

Governor Hogg's only daughter, Miss Ima, presented the site to the State of Texas in 1958. Well known for her patronage of the fine arts, Miss Ima furnished the house with magnificent antiques of the antebellum period. Now open to the public, this oldest plantation in Texas offers a trip back to the days when plantation life was the epitome of gracious living.

The house is actually rather small being only one room deep, and the two rooms on each floor are separated by a wide hall. The downstairs hall, or dog trot, was originally nothing but a dirt floor so a buggy could drive in out of the rain. Now enclosed, the hall floor is covered with a beautiful needlepoint carpet. The historic papers on the walls are the original land grant to Varner and the deed to C. R. Patton.

In the upstairs hallway, Governor Hogg's mementoes are displayed. The Governor was a huge man weighing over 300 pounds, and his over-sized rocking chair was made especially for him by the Huntsville prison inmates. The governor liked to drop in at the prison for meals, and as the officials never knew when to expect him, the quality of the food improved. Grateful inmates presented him with the rocker. There is also an interesting brooch made from the Spindletop well, as the governor held an interest in the gusher.

Rooms are dedicated to eras in Texas history, and the parlor focuses on the Confederacy. The East Room gives emphasis to George Washington with early American pieces. The Pink Room reminds you of a little known part of Texas' past when French refugees settled near Liberty after the fall of Napoleon. Headboards of the beds are made from mahogany bannisters of the old St. Louis Hotel in New Orleans.

A breezeway connects the separate dining room and kitchen that Miss Ima added in the 1920 restoration. The handsome rosewood plantation table is set with Staffordshire "Texian campaigne" china made in England in 1850 to commemorate the Mexican War.

The kitchen looks much as it did when the Hogg family lived here, but back in the days of slavery the kitchen was partitioned into two parts, one for the house and one for the slaves. An old hayfork in the kitchen still stands where the Hogg's cook hung his coat for 40 years.

All plantations had orchards and pecan groves, and it is fitting that pecan trees still flourish at Varner-Hogg Plantation, for it was Governor Hogg who was instrumental in making the pecan tree the state tree of Texas.

The state of Texas is indebted to Miss Ima for many treasured and priceless gifts, and the Varner-Hogg Plantation is one of her most beloved presents to her beloved state.

WEST AND
CENTRAL TEXAS

Harrington House

To some, Texas means cattle and oil, and Amarillo's Harrington House stands as a monument to the best of both industries. Cattlemen John and Pat Landergin built their stately mansion in 1914, and oil industry leaders, Don and Sybil Harrington, preserved and embellished the neoclassic house to the state of artistic achievement we see today. Members of the Panhandle-Plains Historic Society greet visitors warmly and ask them to wear low, broad-heeled shoes during an adventure through this spectacular mansion.

The lowest of the three floors enables us to view the engineering genius that provided comfort way ahead of its time for the original owners. A huge heat-producing boiler stands near bins that once held wood and coal. Adjacent is an Otis elevator, original to the house. Though modern carpet, mirrors, and wall coverings make the elevator's interior plush and elegant, the original mechanical works are visible in the adjoining mechanical room and are still used. On this same floor a large ranch style sitting room boasts photographs of European and American friends of the Harringtons, including the Reagans, the Eisenhowers, and Clark Gable.

The stately residence's main level is beautified with architectural details and enough European and Asian antiques to satisfy any aficionado's palate. A perfectly appointed vestibule introduces visitors to the style and balance found throughout the house. The original front door, 500 pounds of glass and iron, allows natural light for visitors to admire a banquet cushioned with fine 18th-century needlepoint. In the imposing reception room an English needlework rug covers only part of the 18th-century white oak, hand-pegged floors purchased from a chateau in France.

When Mrs. Harrington grew tired of the dark mahogany moldings and facings in the parlor, she had them bleached a lighter color; however, she insisted that the contractor not disturb the silk damask wall coverings which were original to the house. The lovely pale fabric still adorns the walls as beautifully as ever and with not a hint of damage despite the arduous task performed on the woodwork and molding. A collector of fine needlework, Mrs. Harrington takes great pride in the bell pull, fire screen, and chair, needle-pointed by Mr. Harrington's mother.

The continuing interest and artistic expertise of the benefactress graces the entire house but especially is it evident when seasonally she returns to add special touches. Typically, fall decorations can include preserved leaves collected from around the world that lie among the Tiffany china and crystal settings. Long, slender tapers used in the center add a warm glow, and a portrait of the couple's only child, Sally Harrington Goldwater, gazes across the room from above the fireplace. Mrs. Harrington's portrait hangs above the library fireplace; this painting along with many objects d'art affirm the family's taste and interest in the arts. Photographic copies of the family art collection hang throughout the house; the originals were given to a museum in Phoenix, Arizona. Upstairs each of the four bedrooms has special handwork pieces and furniture painstakingly collected for perfect coordination. Most of the original fixtures are in use in each bathroom where light filters through antique lead glass windows.

Near the beginning of the century, cattle built this lovely historic mansion, then oil and gas furnished and embellished it to its present state of grandeur. Today, Mrs. Don Harrington, in the philanthropic tradition of her family, has en-

1600 South Polk
Amarillo 79102
806-374-5490
Hours: 10:00–12:30, Tues. and
Thurs.
2:00–3:30, Sun.
April through Dec.
Limit of 4 per tour
Free admission

dowed and presented her home as a gift to visitors who appreciate superb architecture, antiquity, beauty, and artistry. Harrington House shines like a jewel in the north Texas panhandle, and a trip to Amarillo is worth the journey to see her glitter.

(See color photo.)

The French Legation

802 San Marcos
Austin 78702
512-472-8180
Hours: 1:00–5:00 Tues.–Sun.
Admission charge

Just one block east of Austin's hectic Interstate 35 at 8th Street stands a sturdy survivor of the brief Republic of Texas and a reminder of an Old World culture brought to a new frontier by Comte Alphonse Dubois de Saligny, the French *charge d'affaires.*

On September 25, 1839, King Louis Philippe signed a "Treaty of Amity, Navigation, and Commerce" with the Republic of Texas, and France became the first European nation to recognize the independence of the youngest republic of the New World. From that year until Texas was annexed by the United States in 1846, France maintained diplomatic relations with Texas, although it wasn't easy.

In 1841 a conflict called The Pig War developed between an Austin hotelkeeper, Richard Bullock, and the arrogant Comte. de Saligny complained that Bullock's pigs invaded his stables and even penetrated to his very bedroom to devour the linen and chew his papers. Bullock charged that the Frenchman's servant had killed some of his pigs on orders from his master, so he thrashed the ser-

Here at the French Legation in Austin was the home of the representative of the first nation to recognize the Republic of Texas.

vant and threatened the diplomat himself with a beating. The haughty aristocrat promptly invoked the "Laws of Nations," and claimed diplomatic immunity for himself and his servant and demanded Bullock be punished.

De Saligny was already upset with the administration because it had opposed his project of a Franco-Texian commercial and colonization company. Acting President David Burnet and Secretary of State James Mayfield refused to have the hotelkeeper punished. In a high fit of pique the *charge d'affaires*, without instructions from France, broke diplomatic relations and left Texas in May 1841. From Louisiana de Saligny emitted occasional dire warnings of France's impending retribution, but France had no intention of resorting to force. Finally, when Houston came in office, Texas made "satisfactory explanations," and de Saligny returned in April of 1842, thus ending The Pig War.

The Legation was built on a 21.5-acre tract just outside the boundary of Austin. The Comte paid Anson Jones $1,000 for the property, and the title is dated April 23, 1841, about the time the building was completed. De Saligny lived in the Legation only a short time and sold it to John Odin, later Bishop of the Diocese of Texas. Joseph W. Robertson, Austin's third mayor, purchased the house in 1848, and the Robertson family owned the Legation for 100 years.

This oldest home in Austin was built of Bastrop pine, a fine-grained lumber found nowhere else in the world, and designed in the Louisiana bayou style facing south with a veranda flanked by square pillars. The window glass came from France, and the unusual hardware from England. The large hinges and locks with huge brass knobs and foot-long keys are still unique. Bare plank walls are painted the original colors. Scrapings were taken from the walls, and Pittsburg Paint Company duplicated the pastel colors. Authentic period furniture complete the Legation's perfect restoration, and the snobby Comte would approve of the results.

After the State of Texas purchased the Legation from descendants of the Robertson family, the Daughters of the Republic of Texas obtained custody of this historic property and are responsible for the excellent preservation.

The Governor's Mansion

As you tour the lovely rooms of the Governor's Mansion, it is extremely difficult to believe the State of Texas only appropriated $14,500 to build their chief executive a suitable residence and a mere pittance of $2,500 to furnish it. But, of course, that was way back in 1854 when Austin was a sparsely populated town of about 3,000 citizens, and when Texas had much more land than money.

1010 Colorado
Austin 78701
512-475-2121
Hours: 10:00–12:00 Mon.–Fri.
No admission charge

Austin's masterbuilder, Abner Hugh Cook, submitted the low bid of $14,500 on architect Richard Payne's plans and paid Payne $100 for his design work. Cook came to Texas from Georgia and Tennessee where he learned to build in the Greek Revival style so popular in the south. It is almost certain that Cook copied some of Andrew Jackson's The Hermitage.

In 1856 Governor Elisha and Lucadia Pease moved into what is still considered one of the finest examples of the squarish-columned Greek Revival design. It met the Legislature's requirements for "something that would be an ornament to the Capitol [sic], and creditable as a public building for our rapidly growing state."

Lucadia was not without her housekeeping problems. Rooms sat empty, silverware and crystal were odd sets and pieces, and there was little privacy and no security. However, the governor threw a "levee" in August 1856, and 500 Texans attended to christen the new Executive Mansion.

Texas' next governor did not fair as well. When Sam Houston refused to swear an oath to the Confederacy, the Legislature promptly removed him from office. President Lincoln offered to send troops, but Houston is said to have thrown the letter in the library fireplace. The library's fireplace mantle is the only original one left in the mansion.

With so many famous (and infamous) personages occupying the mansion, many intriguing stories have been passed down through the years. During Pendleton Murrah's residency, his nephew committed suicide over an unrequited love. Governor Hogg had nails driven in the beautiful sweeping banister to keep his sons from sliding down the tempting rail.

The first interior remodeling was done about 1900 under Governor Sayers, and Mrs. Sayers was so proud of the new furnishings, she began public tours of the home. The Colquitts' occupancy was disrupted in 1914 when the only major addition was made with the conservatory and kitchen wing. Colquitt also decided to paint the buff-colored Austin brick white with green blinds so "Texas would have a White House." Colquitt's choice was a winner, and the mansion has stayed white ever since.

State and national history was made when Miriam "Ma" Ferguson became the first woman governor elected in the United States. Of course, "Ma" already knew her way around the mansion because husband James was impeached from the same office.

In 1920 under Governor Hobby, the best addition of all was made to the mansion—the blessed luxury of steam heat. It prompted Dan Moody's wife, Mildred, in 1928 to describe the appearance of the mansion's only ghost. She encountered a "splendid figure" rubbing his hands over one of the new radiators. Recognizing General Sam Houston, she offered him a tour. Houston pooh-poohed the modern conveniences and called the Moodys a pampered lot. Mrs. Moody's tongue-in-cheek tale is the only ghost story about the mansion.

Legislators were notoriously frugal with funds for their chief executive's home. In 1935 lumps of plaster began to fall, and in 1951 a 40-pound section fell where Governor Price Daniel had stood minutes before. There was talk of a new mansion, but Governor John Connally vetoed the $500,000 appropriation. Finally, in 1979 $1 million was appropriated for rehabilitation, and Mrs. Rita Clements founded the Friends of the Governor's Mansion which raised another $2 million.

Many items were donated to the mansion, and one of the outstanding gifts was Robert Onderdonk's "The Fall of the Alamo" painting, found by a Houston family in an antique shop and appraised at $450,000. The twin poster beds in the Pease Bedroom were donated by Pease descendants. Miss Ima Hogg, philanthropist daughter of Governor James Hogg, gave the magnificent dining room table along with numerous other valuable antiques.

The Governor's Mansion is now closer to its own 1856 design than any of the three older governors' residences in the United States. Any Texan that visits this magnificent restoration can be very proud of their governor's home. No matter how exalted the heads of state that are entertained, they will receive a splendid reception in this beautiful mansion.

Neill-Cochran House

Austin's master builder, Abner Cook, was racing against time to complete the Governor's Mansion by December 21, 1855, and avoid paying a late penalty. However, miserable weather and slow deliveries plagued his masterpiece, and the dedicated Abner still had to pay $435 for Governor Pease's rent.

At the same time Cook was absorbed with his major project, he was also building another Greek Revival mansion for wealthy Austinite, Washington Hill. So, it is no surprise that the two houses greatly resemble each other. Whereas the Governor's Mansion has the Ionic columns (Cook felt that Ionic columns were more authoritarian and symbolic of government) the Neill-Cochran House has the Doric columns, which the builder considered more appropriate for a genteel residence. Both houses have the delicate classical balustrade that became Cook's trademark. The Governor's Mansion has been painted white, but the Neill-Cochran walls are still the original limestone rubble even though Cook probably intended them to be plastered. These 18-inch thick walls are secured with mortar mixed with pig bristles, a method thought to give strength and flexibility.

2310 San Gabriel
Austin 78705
512-478-2335
Hours: 2:00–5:00, Wed.–Sun.
Admission charge

The Neill-Cochran House bears a remarkable similarity to the Governor's Mansion in Austin, for they were both constructed by master builder Abner Cook at the same time.

In 1857 this beautiful mansion became the Asylum for the Blind, and during the Civil War it was a hospital. Stories about Federal soldiers buried in the yard are still told. Finally, in 1875, Colonel Andrew Neill, a native of Scotland, purchased the house and returned it to its residential splendor. Neill had practiced law in Seguin, fought in Indian campaigns, and been captured by the Mexican general, Adrian Woll and imprisoned in Mexico. To add to his colorful career, he later became a colonel in the Confederate Army.

In 1892 the estate was sold to Judge T. B. Cochran, and since 1958 the property has belonged to the National Society of Colonial Dames. The restoration of this historic home by this organization is absolutely magnificent.

The many windows of the Neill-Cochran House retain their original wavy, bubbly glass, and as you enter the wide hallway, note the simple, classic lines of the woodwork with its Greek influence. Doorways and windows are slightly wider at their bases, which is architectually pleasing to the eye. Throughout the ground level the hardwood floors were added at the turn of the century by the Cochran family, but the stairs, newel posts, banisters, and upstairs floors are the original Bastrop pine installed by Cook.

A double parlor is separated by massive hung doors rather than the usual sliding doors, and both parlors are beautifully furnished. However, particularly lovely is the Maria Neville Brown French Parlour with its chandelier, candelabra, sconces, and cache pots by Sevres. A Bouille desk and pedestals complement the Sevres porcelain, but the elaborate table with its miniatures on ivory of Madame DuBarry and her contemporaries dominates the exquisite room.

Upstairs are three bedrooms and the library. The library contains many privately printed biographies of Texans, and a unique collection of cookbooks dating from the days of the Republic.

The Colonial Dames were instigators of the movement to select a state flower, and it was the painting of bluebonnets by Miss Mode Walker that influenced the legislature to pass the "Bluebonnet Bill" on March 7, 1901. Miss Walker's painting has a place of honor in the Neill-Cochran House.

The Neill-Cochran House has been judged the third most important structure in Austin by the Texas Historical Commission, and the National Trust for Historic Preservation called it a "jewel and perfect example of the Texas version of the Greek Architectural Revival in the South."

O. Henry House

409 E. 5th
Austin 78701
512-472-1903
Hours: 11:00–4:30, Tues.–Sat.
Free admission

Almost in the shadow of the Capitol sits a small wood frame house that once was the home of one of America's most beloved authors. Although William Sydney Porter was born in North Carolina, he moved to Texas to recover from a bad cough. After two years of working on a ranch near Cotulla, Will felt well enough to head for the big city.

After moving to Austin, Will worked at various jobs and courted the ladies. Finally, he singled out one with the unusual name of Athol, and they eloped in

When he lived in Austin, this was the home of William Sydney Porter, better known as America's favorite short story writer, O. Henry.

1887. The struggling young man lost his job as a draftsman in the land office, and was hired as a teller for the First National Bank of Austin.

Early in 1893 the Porters moved into a modest cottage at 308 E. 4th Street. Athol's health began to fail and Will's job became more and more of a burden. Always the dreamer, Will had difficulty with the bank's books. In hopes of finding a release from the drudgery of the bank, Porter began a weekly newspaper he called *The Rolling Stone*. Here appeared his short stories for the first time in print.

Shortages began to occur at the bank and Will again lost his job. After six months, the writer found a job as a columnist for *The Houston Post*. While in Houston, Will was indicted for embezzlement from the Austin bank, and he fled to Honduras.

More tragedy was in store for Porter. Athol was dying of tuberculosis, and he returned to Austin knowing he would have to face trial. After Athol's death Will was put on trial and yet remained silent throughout the entire proceedings. The weight of evidence sent the 36-year-old Porter to the penitentiary for more than three years. Many believe the writer was innocent.

During those years in prison Porter perfected his craft and adopted the pen name of O. Henry. At his death in New York at age 48, O. Henry had published 381 stories translated into 10 languages.

Even though the 1886 O. Henry house has been moved from its original site, it has been carefully preserved. Several of the Porters' belongings are still intact, which is amazing, as the Porters merely rented the house and never owned it.

The deer horns are from a deer Will shot, and the doll furniture belongs to their daughter. The charming china plates covered with cupids and fruit are Athol's handiwork. Two rocking chairs in the bedroom belonged to Athol's parents. The Porters' bed had passed to a local furniture dealer who displayed it in his store window. One summer, U.T.'s English classes raised the money to buy this O. Henry possession as a gift for the home.

Every Mother's Day, the O. Henry House sponsors a "Pun-Off." Contestants work all year on shaggy dog stories and puns to enter this hilarious event. So, if you are an avid O. Henry fan, sharpen your wits and help support the only monument to this great author's memory.

(See color photo.)

The Browning Plantation

Chappell Hill
Contact: Historic Home Tours of
Chappell Hill
Drawer E
Chappell Hill 77426
409-836-6144
By appointment only
Admission charged

Hanging on the wall of this elegant Greek Revival home is a photograph of an old dilapidated house with gaping holes in the walls and windows falling out, and looking all the world like a huge pile of rotting boards. Incredibly, this wreck and ruin of a house was what Mr. and Mrs. R. P. Ganchan purchased and restored to the now-magnificent Browning Plantation.

Colonel W. W. Browning completed his fine home in 1857. Native cedar was put together with pegs, notched joints, and square nails. With his 2,000 acres and 65 slaves, Browning was a leader in Chappell Hill's civic affairs, and the huge house became a center of activity for many of the social functions associated with the colleges located in the "Athens of Texas." Browning's love for Texas and the Confederacy ran deep, but it brought about his financial downfall. Unconvinced that the South had lost, during the war's final days the Colonel bought worthless Confederate bonds. And, with the freed slaves, his fortune was gone, and his beautiful home was doomed. Not only was his money lost forever, but Browning paid the ultimate price for his loyalty; the life of his only son to the South he loved so dearly.

If this once wealthy plantation owner returned to his home today, it would seem that the more than 130 years since his leaving had never passed, for the Ganchans have not missed a single detail to make the house perfect. You would not be the least surprised if the door opened and a Texas version of Scarlet O'Hara came tripping across the manicured grounds to welcome you inside.

The two-story home has eight rooms, each with a fireplace, and two magnificent halls running the full depth of the house. In the rear of the house, the south veranda has a sweeping view of the gently rolling hills of south Texas. The Ganchans have spared no expense in furnishing their antebellum treasure, and gorgeous antiques of that era add to the beauty of the house.

Downstairs is the parlor, library, and dining room with its authentic *faux boix* (false wood) grained paneling.

Mildred Ganchan can serve a superb lunch to as many as 18 in her grand dining room. Fortunately, however, she doesn't have to cook in the original kitchen which was located 30 feet from the house. It is now attached to the main house and comes equipped with every modern convenience.

On the second story are four handsome bedrooms all furnished in exquisite antiques, and to solve the eternal problem of bathrooms in old houses, the third floor was converted to two huge bathrooms with the men's decorated in mascu-

The 1857 Browning Plantation in Chappell Hill is one of Texas' outstanding restorations.

line bric-a-brac, and the ladies' with somewhat of a bordello look with red decor and mirrored walls.

Shutters rather than curtains cover the tall windows, and walls are painted pastel colors, because wallpaper did not really become fashionable until the Victorian Era.

It is no surprise that the Browning Plantation is a favorite with brides and grooms and the setting for many weddings. Also, the Ganchans open the bedrooms for overnight guests. Texas has many fine restorations, but few have presented such a monumental challenge as the Browning Plantation. The Ganchans deserve very special accolades for their outstanding accomplishment.

The Stagecoach Inn

If ever a town deserved the adjective "tranquil" it is Chappell Hill. Caught in time, historic Chappell Hill was founded in the late 1840s but is believed to have been a trading post long before that. One of the favorite rest stops for persons going to Austin or Waco from Houston was Chappell Hill's Stagecoach Inn. The Inn with its beautiful Greek Revival proportions, its famous victuals, and its relatively luxurious accommodations was a most welcome sight. Built in 1850, the 14-room inn served two stagecoach lines throughout the Civil War. No railroad arrived to save Chappell Hill from fading into oblivion, so what little is left in this charming village dates back to those thriving 1850s.

The two-story inn was sturdily constructed of stone and native cedar, and typical of the period, the entire framework was mortised, tenoned, and pegged. A long rectangular room at the rear of the inn perpendicular to the central entry hall is the only break with the Greek Revival style. It was built as a dining room in which to serve the hungry travelers. Guest rooms were upstairs—each with the added amenity of a washbowl and pitcher.

Chappell Hill
Contact: Historic Home Tours of
Chappell Hill
Drawer E
Chappell Hill 77426
409-836-9515
Tours by appointment only
Admission charge

The Federal influence in the Stagecoach Inn's facade is seen in a central portico that frames the front door in lieu of the usual temple-like veranda. A beautiful Greek key frieze circles the roofline, and the unusual downspout heads dated 1851 bear the Lone Star of Texas.

When there was no longer any use for the Inn, the hostel was totally abandoned. Grapevines created a massive jungle, and rot and decay took over. Talk of razing the landmark was heard in Chappell Hill. Fortunately, in 1976, Houston architect Harvin Moore and his wife, Elizabeth, purchased the pathetic wreck and began its restoration.

After the restoration the Moores added their museum-quality antiques to make the rooms beautiful, yet comfortable, warm, and inviting. Marching up the stairway are Elizabeth's delightful collection of antique doorstops. You want to pick up each one and hear Elizabeth's story about it.

The oversized dining room of the Inn is now a spacious living room with a reproduction of Remington's "The Old Stagecoach of the Plains" hanging over the mantel. A ten-foot pine table from New Ulm displays two clever lamps made of old apothecary jars. Now used as a coffee table, a black stagecoach box, c. 1858, is the perfect touch amidst the superb antiques.

No matter where you look Elizabeth and Harvin have added special appointments. In the upstairs hall an 1830 wagon set was once used to help ladies and children endure rough rides over primitive roads. An Eastlake bed is covered with a signed Pennsylvania coverlet, c. 1839, and the upstairs sitting room boasts a handsome rug braided by Elizabeth. European, New England, and Texas antiques all blend together for a harmonious effect throughout the home. As Elizabeth stresses, the Inn is not a museum, but their home, and there was no reason to duplicate the decor of the Inn as it was so long ago.

Harvin first saw the Stagecoach Inn in 1923 on a band trip while at Rice University. He immediately saw its possibilities and dreamed of owning it. And, 53 years later his dream came true, and he and Elizabeth have created one of the most beautiful and perfect restorations in Texas.

(See color photo.)

McAdams Ranch House

Approximately one mile beyond end of Ranch Road 654 which extends south of US 70 between Crowell and Paducah.
Contact: Betty Gafford
Box 609
Crowell, TX 79227
Donations

It is not easy to find the McAdams Ranch House. In fact, you've got to really want to go there. You feel like you're on the road to nowhere, but persevere, for it is well worth the trip. And, best of all, you get to meet the owner, Betty Gafford.

Betty's grandfather, crusty J. J. McAdams built the house in 1917 at the peak of his success as a rancher. J. J. had a violent temper and at the height of an argument, murdered his brother. Amazingly enough, he was acquitted of the crime.

The cattle business has always operated on a boom or bust basis, and by 1921 J. J. was busted. Wonderful stories are told how the rancher warded off creditors by meeting them at the door with a shotgun. That same year J. J. was the victim of a stroke, and the house passed to his son Leslie.

Leslie was a great music lover, and Betty remembers many evenings when the strains of her father's violin would mix with the accompanying piano. Leslie and

his wife hosted many parties and dances, and the house was filled with guests. Sometimes Leslie brought in a ten-piece orchestra to play for the soirees.

When Leslie and his wife died, the house seemed to die with them. It soon took on the look of all neglected empty houses. Paint peeled away, the roof sagged and leaked, and even the windows seemed hollow and bleak. Betty seriously considered tearing her old home down, but her husband, Otis and other friends and neighbors who all had many rememberances of happy times protested. Finally, Betty and Otis decided to restore the house.

Otis set to work making repairs, repainting, and rebuilding. Betty began striping away old cracked varnish and applying new finishes to the wonderful antique furniture. Flea markets and antique shops were scoured for special treasures and replacements for broken pieces. Neighbors dropped by to inspect the progress, and soon donations of furniture and bric-a-brac began to pour in. So many fine items were given that Otis converted the front porch to a display room, which includes, strangely enough, Lee Harvey Oswald's can opener. Oswald's mother was employed by the Gaffords during the time Oswald was in Russia. (See *Amazing Texas Monuments and Museums*, Lone Star Books, Houston, Texas, 1984.)

Now, the ranch house displays the prosperous lifestyle of a rancher at the turn of the century. In the parlor, with its heavy Victorian pieces, is J. J.'s infamous rifle mounted above the front door, and his obituary framed above the fireplace. Leslie's beloved Italian violin rests beside the grand piano.

The richly trimmed dining room table is set with Golden Pheasant china, beautiful cut glass, and a Madeira tablecloth that add to the elegance of the room. Leslie's belt buckle, spurs, and tie clasp are mounted on black velvet and hang from the wall.

Mannequins pose gracefully in their splendid turn-of-the-century costumes, and every room looks ready for one of Leslie's famous parties. One piece that seems out of place is the rocking chair in the kitchen. No rancher's wife ever had time to sit down and rock with all those kitchen chores waiting for her.

Betty Gafford epitomizes Texas hospitality with, "The door is open just anytime someone wants to come out and look." While Crowell is not exactly on the beaten path, if you are ever up that way, don't miss one of Texas' best tributes to home on the range.

Magoffin Home

It was an exciting time for the Magoffin family when in 1856 young Joseph returned from his Kentucky schooling to join his father and brother in their trading post opposite Juarez on the Rio Grande River. The father, James Wiley Magoffin, had recently ended the somewhat humorous Salt War skirmish during which he had "invaded" New Mexico, and local citizens were devising plans at the Magoffin home for repelling Indian marauders who were raiding local corrals. In short, the Old West was experiencing growing pains. In spite of all the problems, the Magoffin family trading business flourished. Travelers replenished their worn-out stock by purchasing mules from them by the hundreds, and the

1120 Magoffin Ave.
El Paso 79901
915-533-5147
Hours: 9:00 till 4:00, Wed. through
Sun.
Admission charge

family wagon trains brought commodities needed by the community from the ports of the Gulf Coast. Then in 1861 Texas seceded from the Union; and though the Magoffins were not slave owners, they did support Texas, so Joseph fought as a commissioned major in the Confederacy.

Like many other southerners, the family lost all its property during Reconstruction days, and it took appeals on two separate trips to Washington to regain their holdings. Nonetheless, with the property intact, Joseph threw himself into a busy career of politics and commerce. While serving four times as mayor of El Paso and seeing his various business enterprises flourish as well, the younger Magoffin built his spacious adobe home and reestablished the social traditions of his parents. The house again became the setting for receptions, dances, and spectacular anniversary celebrations for Joseph and his Hispanic wife, Octavia.

The Magoffin home is one of the few remaining examples of Territorial architecture in Texas. Thick adobe walls, a U-shaped floor plan, and interior courtyard are traditional Spanish styles. But many Eastern motifs were used as well, i.e., Greek Revival symmetrical doors and windows and the Roman pillar-like facades on some of the fireplaces. The size of the banquet table, which easily seats 40 diners, testifies to the grand style of Magoffin soirees which at times extended through the night and included breakfast the next morning. The chairs reflect a blending of styles. The native craftsmen used the formal Eastlake cushioned seats, backs, and arms but featured a carved Mexican eagle plus a horseshoe on the crest of each chair.

Waiting to be viewed by posterity, The Magoffin House remains nestled among stately Italian cypress trees on the corner of the streets bearing the names of its first master and mistress, Magoffin and Octavia.

Mrs. Sam Houston's House

Independence
Contact: The Mrs. Sam Houston
House
Rt. 5, Box 105
Independence, Texas 77833
409-830-1959
713-666-2575
Hours: Reservations only
Admission charge

A stately, two-story house stands on the crest of a hill in the tiny hamlet of Independence. One of the earliest surviving Greek Revival houses in Texas, the house with its simple portico and white columns faces the remnants of the town square. Built in the 1830s by John Bancroft Root, the house was constructed of hand-hewn cedar and remains virtually unchanged today. It was this pleasant home that Margaret Moffette Lea Houston purchased for herself and eight children, following the death of her husband Sam Houston in 1863.

Margaret met Sam Houston at her brother's home in Mobile, Alabama, in May of 1839. She was 20 years old. When he left for Texas a week later, she had promised to become his wife, and they were married a year later. An ardent and devoted Baptist, it was through her efforts that General Houston joined the Baptist church. Margaret's public life was that of a wife of a great political figure, but privately, she wrote poetry and love letters to her husband.

General and Mrs. Sam Houston had a busy bustling household of eight children, but at Houston's death, none had reached his majority. Therefore, Margaret moved from her husband's home in Huntsville to be near her mother in Independence. Back in those days Baylor was the best university in Texas and was located in the thriving town of Independence. It was here Margaret planned on educating her children. Sadly, Margaret only survived her husband by four years. In 1867 an epidemic of yellow fever swept through Texas, and she became one of its last victims on December 3. It was against the law to transport bodies killed by the fever, so Margaret was unable to be buried next to her beloved Sam. She rests in the cemetery of the Baptist Church in Independence.

Margaret's crepe myrtles still bloom in the front yard, and the house is much the same as when she and her brood lived here. Over 150 years old, the house is still sound, but the front porch had to be completely restored. It was from this banister that a white bed sheet was hung when Margaret died. The wall-to-wall carpet was removed and underneath were many surprises. A "milk paint" (a milk-base paint containing animal blood) had to be cleaned—*and cleaned*—all by hand. Wooden pegs, cut nails, tin can lids, square pegs, and lots of hammered copper were found in the old floors.

Margaret gave a lavish reception in her house on August 1, 1866, when her eldest daughter married Captain Joseph Clay Stiles Morrow, with 300 of Texas' finest crowding into her house. Just two months later, her second daughter and namesake, "Maggie," married LaFayette Williams with a quiet ceremony. On June 4, 1867, the first grandchild of Sam and Margaret Houston was born in the upper east bedroom. She was Margaret Houston Morrow, the only grandchild Margaret was ever to see.

Maggie Williams and her family lived in the house until 1898. During this period Sam Houston, Jr., returned home to live out his years in this house, and he, too, is buried in Independence.

A few of the Williams' furnishings are still there, but most of the pieces have been added by the owner, Frankie Slaughter. At the time of Margaret's death, Santa Anna's saddle and snuff box were in her possession, but have long ago gone to other museums.

Perhaps it is fitting that Margaret Houston's final resting place is in Independence, a place she once called, ". . . thou loveliest spot on earth to me." Her last home, now listed on the National Register of Historic Places stands as an enduring tribute to "Texas' First First Lady."

N. W. Faison Home

In September of 1842, Santa Anna sent General Adrian Woll to capture San Antonio. When news of the invasion reached La Grange, Nicholas Mosby Dawson assembled a group of men to help Matthew Caldwell route the Mexicans from Texas. Dawson marched his 53 men toward the Salado River where he was discovered by a detachment of Mexicans. The Texans prepared to fight, but the Mexicans brought up two pieces of artillery and soon killed Dawson and 35 of his gallant volunteers. Of the 15 captured, 3 escaped and the rest were marched to Mexico City and held in Perote Prison. Only 9 of the 12 prisoners came back to

822 S. Jefferson Street
La Grange 78945
409-968-5532
Hours: 2:00–5:00, Sun., April
through August
Admission charge

Here in La Grange, in the shadow of Monument Hill where the volunteers killed in the Mier and Dawson Expeditions are buried, is the home of one of the Dawson survivors, N. W. Faison.

Texas. One of the fortunate 9 was N. W. Faison who was pardoned by Santa Anna and worked to have the remains of his comrades returned as well.

Faison was successful, and today the bodies of those martyred men rest in a common tomb on Monument Hill overlooking the little town of La Grange. They share their grave with the victims of the infamous Black Bean Incident in Mier, Mexico. (See "Walter Paye Lane," *Unsung Heroes of Texas*, Lone Star Books, Houston, 1986.)

Faison was a surveyor by trade but also served as a county clerk. He was born in 1817 in North Carolina but came to Fayette County in 1837. The hero of the Dawson Massacre died a bachelor in 1870. His home serves as a reminder of his heroism in defending his adopted Texas.

In 1961 three women had the foresight to recognize the historical significance of the Faison home. Having only $20 in the treasury, the La Grange Garden Club, with inspired ingenuity and enthusiasm raised the $5,500 necessary to buy the home, and that included all of the furniture. With the leadership of Mrs. Gladys Flournoy, Mrs. Verna Reichert, and Mrs. Marguerite Willmann, restoration began.

Using the design inspired by a local nurseryman, G. B. Mueller, the Garden Club incorporated 53 black tiles on the stone terrace of the home: 36 to commemorate the Dawson men and 17 to commemorate the Mier men who drew black beans and were executed. A local lumber company and brick yard donated their products, and gifts from local citizens began to arrive. Among the donations were paintings, bric-a-brac, carpets, and a wonderful bedspread made by Mississippi plantation slaves. It is sewn in three sections so it could be ripped apart to fit in a tub and washed over an open fire.

The lamp in the entry looks like it came straight from a Mexican market, but actually it dates back to 1700 or 1800. A delightful painting of members of the Faison family hangs in the hall, but the artist is unknown. Oddly, none of the original paintings in the house are signed.

Against the wall in the charming little parlor is a heavy square Knobe piano that originally cost several thousand dollars when it was purchased, truly a hefty price at the turn of the century. The red velvet chair with its biscuit tuffing is built on an iron pipe frame, and the unusual glass case with its little gimcracks is an old gun case.

The N. W. Faison House and its restoration is a wonderful tribute to the La Grange Garden Club and its dedicated members who worked so hard to preserve a part of Texas' history.

Ranching Heritage Center

When you visit the Ranching Heritage Center and trace the history of ranching in Texas with its authentic houses, barns, school, and even a gigantic old steam engine, you will be impressed with the hard work and perseverance it took to settle the Great Plains. These pioneer buildings have been moved to the Center intact from all parts of Texas' Great Plains. Particularly memorable are the primitive abodes the pioneers called home, and here at the Ranching Heritage Center you can easily visualize the incredible hardships of life on the frontier and appreciate their enduring courage.

Texas Tech University
Box 4349
Lubbock 79409
806-742-1498
Hours: 9:00–4:30, Mon.–Sat.
1:00–4:30, Sun.
Free admission

El Capote Cabin (1838)

Imagine how hard life must have been in the crude El Capote Cabin with its hand-hewn log walls chinked with a crude mud mixture. Rain leaked through the hand-split shingled roof, and puncheons (boards finished on only one side) made up the floor. The simple stone fireplace was used for cooking, heating, and light, and furnishings were sparse (not even a bed) and all poorly handmade.

Hedwig Hill Cabin (1853)

This double log cabin represents the German ethnic influence in frontier Texas. It consists of two log cabins joined by a breeze-way called a dog trot which provided a cool living area during the hot Texas summers. The upstairs rooms were used for sleeping and storage.

Unlike the El Capote Cabin, the furnishings demonstrate the Germans' fine craftsmanship. The kitchen corner table is an example of the Briedermeier style (see "Andreas Breustedt House," New Braunfels) with its simple form and characteristic curved legs.

The Hedwig Hill Cabin is twin cabins with an open breeze-way called a dog trot between them.

Box And Strip House (1903)

Up on the treeless high plains lumber was practically nonexistent and expensive to obtain. So a simple box was constructed of 1 × 12 boards nailed to a frame with 1 × 4 strips nailed over the cracks. However, lack of insulation made these houses dreadfully uncomfortable.

Typical settlers were large families who occupied box and strip dwellings, and furnishings in this house depict the tasks of the ranch wife. The kitchen table had drawers lined with metal for flour and sugar. A cabinet with pierced tin panels to allow for air circulation was used to store bread and pies. Without any access whatsoever to stores, most of the furnishings had to be ordered from catalogs.

Harrell House (1803–1917)

As families and fortunes grew, ranch homes were added on to and improved. The Harrell House began as a tiny stone structure which grew into a large T-shaped house, as two box and strip additions were added later. Furnishings acquired from distant factories in the East reflect the lifestyle of the middle income rancher. Note the telephone. What a treat it must have been when it was installed!

Picket and Sotol House (1904–1905)

This rough type of dwelling was widely used by settlers in Southwest Texas where sotol was prevalent. Two rooms were constructed of sotol stalks (the flower

The Pickett and Sotol House at Lubbock's Ranching Heritage Center is typical of the pioneers' use of the land for building a home. The stalks of the sotol plant were the material used for this dwelling's walls.

stalks of yucca-like plants). Cedar posts were placed upright 4 feet apart and the sotol stalks nailed on horizontally to both sides. Rocks and rubble were used for insulation,and the roof was thatched with sacahuiste, another variety of yucca. The picket room was built by placing cedar posts upright in a trench and nailing them to a 2 × 4 at the top. With its dirt floor, the picket and sotol house was as basic a home as the pioneers could have.

Barton House (1909)

By the turn of the century, some ranchers began to acquire wealth and social status, which of course required a mansion. J. J. Barton heard that the railroad

The 1909 Barton House at Lubbock's Ranching Heritage Center is representative of early Texas ranchers' homes.

would pass through his property, so he founded the town of Bartonsite, and built his huge Victorian home. Unfortunately, the railroad chose another route, and Bartonsite's residents moved to Abernathy, leaving the mansion high and dry. The house was left to the museum by the second generation Mrs. Barton, but without funding for its restoration. Over $250,000 was spent to get the house in its present condition, but it is now a real highlight of the Ranching Heritage Center.

With its mansard-style roof and captain's walk, the Barton House is an outstanding example of Victorian domestic architecture. It was built with the fantastic luxuries of running water and a bathroom. Furnishings recreate a genteel lifestyle and the lovely wallpapers throughout Barton House are reproductions of those originally used.

Originally a dugout, this basic cabin at the Ranching Heritage Center was the lonely home for a section manager and his family on a large ranch.

Even though all of the buildings and homes were moved to the Ranching Heritage Center from different parts of Texas, the landscaping is so well done, it is hard to believe they are not on their original sites. A stroll through this outstanding museum is a stroll through a part of Texas' history that created the legends and lore of the Texas mystique.

(See color photo.)

Highlands Mansion

In the "gay nineties" when cotton reigned in the fertile Brazos River bottom land, Basil C. Clark, a Civil War veteran, banker, and cotton king, married a wealthy widow named Mrs. Sally Robinson. As a wedding gift for his new bride, Clark planned to build the most elegant house in the area. Great attention was given the smallest detail to create a Victorian house with a definite European flare. At the turn of the century, the construction was complete and the "Highlands" was rightfully proclaimed overwhelming and noble. Unfortunately, the first mistress was not to live out her life here; the couple had enjoyed their home only fifteen years when Mr. Clark committed suicide in the abode he had presented as a gift to his bride. Seven years later the twice widowed woman sold Highlands Mansion and moved to California, never to see her home again.

Over the next 50 years the house changed hands three times. By 1964 the house had deteriorated almost beyond repair when Mr. and Mrs. Lee Loeffler of Houston purchased it and began restoration. The Thomas Michalskys next bought the old home and completed the work.

Visitors, invited in the side door, experience a feeling of total grandeur at first entry into this majestic Victorian home. The rooms are immense with proportional furniture, doors, and windows, all finished with meticulous detailing. Tranquility and dignity best describe the mood of the dining room with its original quartered oak dining table and built-in lighted china cabinet. Beveled and cut glass doors with silver-plated hardware reveal beautiful antique bone china within.

As you enter the breathtaking Great Room, your eyes dart from the oversized red banquet in the center of the room, to the domed ceiling two and a half stories high, and then to the 12 foot tall fireplace as you absorb the grandeur of a chamber that can best be described as awesome. Light filters through the stained glass dome where the bow and wreath design gracefully connects one colorful cherub to another. Several museum-quality pieces belong to the house, and near the front

Highway 147 East
Marlin 76661
817-883-5234
Hours: 10:00–4:00, Mon.–Sat.
1:00–4:00, Sun.
Admission charge

Highlands Mansion's original owner, Basil Clark, succeeded in his dream to build the most elegant home in the area around Marlin. Almost a century later the glorious old mansion may still claim that same title.

door we see the first, an early American clock which has a "moon face." On full moon nights, the clock's moon is above the 12.

In contrast to the darker, paneled portions of the house, the pastel twin parlors contain fine gold leaf French furniture and a 100-year-old rosewood square grand piano made in Philadelphia. While the Victorian ladies were chatting in the parlors, the gentlemen retired upstairs to the smoking room which still has its tucked and buttoned leather walls. China bowl pipes hang crossed above the fireplace and are duplicated in a design painted on each of the ceiling's four corners.

So perfectly was the Highlands Mansion planned that to the present day no structural changes have been necessary, thus visitors know they are seeing an elegant Victorian home exactly as it was intended. Mr. and Mrs. Thomas A. Michalsky, present owners, invite you to share the splendor of their exquisite Highlands Mansion, sitting regally amid sweeping lawns of manicured boxwood hedges and 52 gentle live oak trees. This living jewel still shines brightly and invites you to share in Victorian splendor and glitz as it was enjoyed in the gay nineties.

(See color photo.)

The Seaquist Home

400 Broad Street
Mason 76856
Contact: Mrs. Clara Seaquist
915-347-5413
Hours: Reservations only
Admission charge

On the edge of the Hill Country, just before the endless horizons of the plains begin, is one of Texas' most charming towns. Picturesque Mason is also headquarters for rock hounds searching for the elusive state stone, the Texas topaz. Right off the town square is the majestic Seaquist Home, and if there were a governor of West Texas, you can bet he would make this impressive house his executive mansion.

As are many of Mason's buildings that give the town its special charm, the Seaquist Home is constructed of hand-carved native sandstone. The 3-story mansion with its 17 rooms and 14 fireplaces, and its turrets, gables, and numerous columns is certainly the most predominant edifice in town. One fireplace is large enough to burn 4-foot logs, and its hearthstone is a massive, solid, 10-foot slab of sandstone. It is said that it took a team of six mules to haul this huge stone to the fireplace.

The handsome walnut shutters are handmade, and many of the windows are stained "jewel" glass set with polished minerals and rocks. When the West Texas sun streams through the gorgeous panes, it creates a "jewel" effect on the polished stones. All of the woodwork and wainscoating, as well as the beautiful staircase with its hand-carved newel post is of solid walnut. There are no nails whatsoever in this unique staircase.

Not only does the Seaquist Home have a full basement, which is certainly unusual in Texas, but there is also a card room, a billiard room, and as all mansions should definitely have, a ballroom. The curved archway in the upper story ballroom has caused many an architect to be amazed as to how the rocks were set in place long enough for the mortar to set.

E. M. Reynolds, who built this house in the 1890s, had his name etched on one of the front doors, and the family lived in their palatial home more than 25 years.

In 1919 the house was sold to Oscar Seaquist, a talented bootmaker who arrived in Mason from Sweden in 1901. Oscar married Miss Ada Garner who spent her life working with loving care to preserve her beautiful home. Ada did her work well, and her son, Garner, and his wife, Clara, still live in this magnificent story-book mansion.

(See color photo.)

The Castle

A tour through the marvelous old Castle is a tour of the perfect Victorian house. Not only is the architecture marvelous with its bays, turret, stained glass windows, and gables, but inside is a Victorian grande dame's dream come true. Every spare inch of space is filled with a delightful treasure.

Every bibelot has a story. Tim's wonderful old family Bible begun April 10, 1878, graces the main parlor. Two dolls in long lacy baby dresses in a dear little buggy are actually wearing Helen's mother's and aunt's real baby dresses. The porcelain dolls are reproductions that Helen has hand-painted and dressed. All around are pieces of *capa de monte* porcelain that Helen collects.

The sailor suit on the ancient little mannikin in the small parlor was Helen's father's World War I navy uniform cut down to fit her brother when they did a tap dance together. Helen found the mannikin in Colorado and brought him home on the plane.

When the Urquharts bought the Castle every room was beige on beige, drab with no personality, and very un-Victorian. Now the walls are bright dynamic colors and show off Helen's bric-a-brac to full advantage. The dining room is exceptionally lovely with its stenciled walls and ceiling. Helen's oak dining room table and eight chairs match the oak woodwork perfectly.

1403 East Washington
Navasota 77868
Contact: Helen and Tim Urquhart
409-825-8051
Hours: Reservations only. Minimum of 10 people.
Admission charge

A tour through Navasota's "Castle" is a tour of the perfect Victorian house.

The large entry hall has a very handsome marquetry floor with five different woods. Tim builds charming replicas of old buildings, and several are here in the entry. The Tiffany-style lamp was one of the few fixtures in the house the Urquharts kept. A beautiful stairway leads to four bedrooms that the Urquharts feature as a bed and breakfast. Each is furnished in wonderful antiques and offers very romantic accommodations. The magnificent stained glass windows are replicas of those blown out in the storm of 1900.

Throughout the entire Castle all of the panes are beveled glass, even down to the little door on the outside fuse box. And the Castle probably had one of the first garbage disposals. A Majestic brand cast iron garbage receiver allowed the cook to send the garbage right outside to be picked up by the garbage man. Also built in was a "jealous husband" model porcelain ice box. This huge nickle-trimmed box was loaded from the outside, so the iceman never came in the kitchen.

All of these modern conveniences were built in 1893 by Ward Templeman as a wedding present to his bride, Annie Foster. Local craftsmen used the now-extinct curly pine throughout the house. In 1910 the house was bricked, and the porch was glassed in with 110 panes of beveled glass.

This wonderful mansion had become a haunted house in the 1930s, totally abandoned. It had been given to the Presbyterian Church, but the senior citizens who lived there were unable to climb the stairs. It last belonged to an old bachelor who sold off much of the property and let the house go to rack and ruin. The Castle required a major restoration project for all of the wiring, and the roof had to be replaced and heating and airconditioning added. Thanks to the Urquharts The Castle is once again the fine home that Ward Templeman built for his Annie.

Andreas Breustedt House (Museum of Texas Handmade Furniture)

Conservation Plaza
1370 Church Hill Dr.
New Braunfels 78130
512-629-6504
Hours: Memorial Day through Labor
Day:
10:00–4:00, Tues.–Sat.
1:00–4:00, Sun.
Labor Day through Memorial
Day:
10:00–4:00, Sat. and Sun.
only
Admission charge

When the German colonists arrived in Texas they did not leave behind their Old World customs, nor all of the comforts of home. Between 1845 and 1847 about 7,000 settlers came from Germany, and 46 were listed as cabinetmakers. They plied their trade well, and to appreciate their fine craftsmanship, visit the 1858 Andreas Breustedt House, or as it is commonly known, the Museum of Texas Handmade Furniture.

W. H. Dillen and his wife began collecting these rare pieces of furniture when they moved to New Braunfels in 1945. Now, thanks to the Dillens, some 75 excellent samples of early German workmanship dating from the mid-19th century to the late 1860s are on display.

Some of the earliest pieces were influenced by the Biedermeier style, which was very popular in Europe in the middle 1830s. German royalty copied the French Empire style, and the affluent middle class wanted something similar.

Panhandle-Plains Historical Society

Perhaps the grandest spectacle on the Panhandle Plains is Amarillo's elegant Harrington House with its indoor fountain, stained glass bathroom windows, and silk damask walls (p. 63).

If there were a governor of West Texas, he would probably want to make the impressive Seaquist Mansion in Mason his official dwelling (p. 82).

M. Murphy/Texas Tourist Development Agency

Barton House at Lubbock's Ranching Heritage Center must have looked out of place when it was constructed in 1909 on the lone prairie of West Texas (p. 77).

As you climb the steep, narrow stairs of the John Jay French House in Beaumont, you find a bedroom-nursery filled with dear little treasures for children of a bygone age (p. 39).

Along with his home, John Jay French built many outbuildings, and his little settlement became known as French Town (p. 39).

Beaumont Historical Society

Mrs. John J. French had the first house in Beaumont made of lumber and the first home that was painted (p. 39).

Using old photographs as a guide, the Galveston Historical Foundation has been able to authentically furnish the grand Italianate mansion of Ashton Villa (p. 44).

R. Reynolds/Texas Tourist Development Agency

Here at beautiful Ashton Villa, the romance and gaiety of Victorian Galveston lingers on (p. 44).

R. Reynolds/Texas Tourist Development Agency

One of Texas' great unsung heroes and a financier of the Republic, Sam Williams, built his modest home in Galveston (p. 47).

Port Arthurians refer to their beautiful Pompeiian Villa as the "three-billion dollar villa," because an entrepreneur traded his new Texaco stock (later worth $3 billion) for the mansion (p. 56).

Port Arthur's millionaire, Isaac Ellwood, planned to furnish his Pompeiian Villa with antiques, so furnishings were chosen to reflect Ellwood's intentions (p. 56).

Many of Port Arthur's citizens donated fine antiques to restore Pompeiian Villa to its present splendor (p. 56).

A highlight of Port Arthur's Pompeiian Villa is the four gorgeous antique panels depicting "Spring," "Summer," "Fall" and "Winter" (p. 56).

Many important figures in Texas history, from Captain Zebulon Pike to Sam Houston, were received in these rooms of the Spanish Governor's Palace (p. 89).

One of the few remaining buildings from the centuries of Spanish rule is the Spanish Governor's Palace in San Antonio (p. 89).

Texas Tourist Development Agency

One of the charming stops on Chappell Hill's tour of fine old historic homes is Waverly (p. 107).

R. Reynolds/Texas Tourist Development Agency

Tiny Chappell Hill was once an important town on a stage route through Texas, and its Stagecoach Inn a welcome respite (p. 71).

Texas Highways

The 1939 Rancho Encinal was to "look 100-years-old upon completion," and the result was one of Dallas' most beautiful homes (p. 5).

*The Beaux Arts Colonial
McFaddin-Ward House is as
magnificent today as it was in 1907
(p. 40).*

*Victorian opulence at its height is
brilliantly displayed in the
gorgeous conservatory of the
McFaddin-Ward Mansion (p. 40).*

*America's only shrine to one of its most
beloved authors, O. Henry, is this plain
frame home in Austin (p. 68).*

Totally surrounded by Brownsville's busy downtown, the 1850 Greek Revival Stillman House is an anachronism in the land of adobe (p. 106).

M. Murphy/Texas Tourist Development Agency

R. Reynolds/Texas Tourist Development Agency

The Nichols-Rice-Cherry House in Houston's Sam Houston Park is a highlight on the Christmas Candlelight Tour (p. 50).

R. Reynolds/Texas Tourist Development Agency

The delightful Pillot House in Sam Houston Park was occupied by the Pillot family from 1868 to 1964 (p. 50).

Papa Biedermeier was a cartoon character, so the royalty, in jest, called the middle class imitations "Biedermeier furniture." A corner cupboard here in the house executed by master craftsman Johann Michael Jahn is of Biedermeier design.

Each room of the house holds a treasure of antiques. Expert cabinetmaker Franz Stautzenberger crafted a beautiful draw leaf walnut dining table and a dear little child's chair of mesquite with a seat and back splat of elm. Woods used were mostly walnut and pine, and the pine had to come from Bastrop, 60 miles away.

Also on display in this jewel of a house is an extensive collection of English ironstone dinnerware mass produced in England for the American market from 1842 to 1865.

For these hard-working and courageous colonists who came to this harsh and alien land, a lovely handmade chair or table was much more than a piece of furniture. It was a cherished memory of home.

Also part of Conservation Plaza is the 1852 Baetge House which also has a fine collection of handmade furniture. The second floor is unfurnished, but a section of the wall is exposed so you can appreciate its *fachwerk* construction. (See "Lindheimer House.")

Carl Baetge was commissioned by the czarina of Russia to build the first railroad connecting Moscow with St. Petersburg. While he was overseeing the construction, Baetge met one of the young ladies-in-waiting to the czarina. She was 19, and Carl was 42 when they married in 1846. By 1850 they were in New Braunfels, and one wonders how the young Frau Baetge felt after leaving the 1,050-room Russian palace for this humble cottage in a foreign land. Carl must have been a man of great charm indeed.

Other buildings once threatened with destruction are part of New Braunfels' Conservation Plaza and all delightfully depict the German heritage of Texas.

Lindheimer Home

Only a real Texas history buff would recognize the name of the "Father of Texas Botany," yet Ferdinand Lindheimer's name was given to more than 30 varieties of Texas plants, including *opuntia lindheimer*, or the common prickly pear.

Lindheimer's colorful career in Texas began when this refugee from Prussian politics arrived one day too late to aid Sam Houston in the rout of Santa Anna on April 21, 1836. So, without the reward of a soldier's land grant, Lindheimer began roaming the wilds of Texas collecting plants the world had never seen before. Botanical gardens and Harvard University were avid markets, and their leading botanists rewarded Lindheimer by adding his name to his discoveries.

In 1844, because of his knowledge of the Texas wilderness, Prince Carl of Solms-Braunfels hired the botanist to guide his German colonists to their land grant on the Comal River. For his invaluable service to Prince Carl, Lindheimer was rewarded with a plot of ground. He built a small cottage, but planted a large garden, and the street became New Braunfels' Garden Street.

491 Comal
New Braunfels
Contact: P.O. Box 933
        New Braunfels 78130
        512-525-8766
Hours: Sept.–April: 2:00–5:00,
        Sat.–Sun.
        May–Aug.: 2:00–5:00, daily
Admission charge

This small quaint fachwerk *cottage in New Braunfels was the home of Ferdinand Lindheimer, "the father of Texas botany."*

Lindheimer married Elenore Reinarz in 1846 and enlarged his cabin for her home. Constructed of *fachwerk*, a medieval method of building, a framework of studs and braces was pegged together on the ground and then raised into place. Rocks and homemade bricks were used to fill in between the timbers. Lindheimer's descendants lived in this well-built home until the 1960s when his granddaughter, Mrs. Sida Simon, gave the home to the New Braunfels Conservation Society.

When you visit the Lindheimer Home, note a hand-hewn case holding pieces of type and framed copies of the *New Braunfelser Zeitung*. The former botanist, feeling a newspaper helped the German community understand its role in the new Republic, began printing one himself. An avid supporter of the Confederacy, Lindheimer angered the anti-slavery town, and his printing press was thrown in the Comal River. Lindheimer fished it out and went right on printing the war news. No paper was available, so he used his scant supply of silk tissues saved for his plant specimens.

Many of the original furnishings are still in the cottage. The large walnut desk was crafted by Ebensberger, a fine cabinet maker of the area, and the swan rocker is by the master craftsman Johann Jahn.

Lindheimer's friends remain in the house, too. A fine original sketch of Pestalozzi with a personal note to Lindheimer is here as well as a drawing of Mozart. How strange these portraits must have looked on the rude Texas frontier, yet Lindheimer was not just a botanist and printer, but a student of law, the arts, and languages. He had been a professor in Germany and was a cousin of the great Goethe. How lonely Lindheimer must have been for intellectual conversation during his life in Texas.

As you drive Texas' highways and enjoy the panoply of wild flowers and native plants, give a thought to botanist Ferdinand Lindheimer who contributed so much to his new homeland.

Henkel Square

When Mrs. Faith Bybee and her late husband, Charles L. Bybee, drove to Round Top to inspect the land and settlement of old houses he had bought sight-unseen, she said to him, "You haven't bought yourself anything but a grove of oak trees." According to Mrs. Bybee, her husband would not have minded that for he "did have a love for groves of trees," but the deteriorating dwellings she had found so discouraging at first proved to be the perfect challenge for these ardent historical preservationists. Mrs. Bybee and her late husband have created a living classroom in Round Top where interested visitors can study the lifestyle of early Texans. Henkel Square, the "classroom," is actually a settlement where this "guardian angel of authenticity" continues her restoration of buildings to depict how the Anglo/American and German/American settlers lived in this small community in the 19th century.

When the first Anglo/American pioneers settled the area, they lived in hastily constructed brush arbors or in the same covered wagons that brought them into Texas. Eventually time permitted the building of pioneer houses, now preserved in this tiny community. Early Round Top, named for a house with a round top used as a lookout for Indians, probably sprang up around a plantation commissary operated to care for the slaves. Many eastern colonial settlers were lured to Texas by the promise of cheap or free land, while the port of Galveston provided easy access for families immigrating from Europe in search of freedom. Seeking to escape an oppressive czar, the Henkel family fled their native Germany and had built a new home in Texas by about 1851.

To enter the settlement, you must first pass through the quaint Apothecary Shop to the square itself. The Henkel House, for which the restoration project was named, remains in its original location. The hand blown window panes and some of the furnishings are similar to those used by the original owners. The baby bed, two chests, and a most unusual reclining chair were the ones actually used by the Henkel family. In one room you can still see the barely visible strawberry design stenciled by the artist, Melchior. Four layers of wallpaper were removed to reveal the original; then again in the interest of purism, a Boston firm was engaged to reproduce an exact copy.

On around the square you see Texas' first double log house built by a Mr. Muckelroy, a Tennessee man who followed his much-admired friend Sam Houston to Texas. Another house on the square belonged to Mr. Steeler, who was rewarded for choosing to settle in Sam Houston's Texas by being made the state's first surveyor. The early settlement of Round Top had many small buildings including a church, built by Mr. Henkel and still in use today, an organ manufacturing shop, and a tin maker's shop. Later additions included a candy store, a dress shop, and a cobbler's shop where shoes were custom cast and made. Perhaps the best evidence of the German influence will be seen in the two breweries under restoration. A Houston man donated the barn that has become a lecture hall or "Theatre Barn" used for programs to study life as it was lived then. Much of the small village is finished while some buildings are in various stages of restoration. At completion the project will be a 62-structure settlement, well worth a full day's tour. The aspirations of this grande dame of Texas are even now realized when elderly people come to sit on the porches of Henkel Square to enjoy the feelings and memories of their childhood. She hopes to stir the interest of younger Texans with the

P.O. Box 82
Round Top 78954
409-249-3308
Hours: 12:00–5:00, daily
  Closed Christmas,
    Thanksgiving, Easter,
    Mother's Day
Admission charge

leaflets telling the stories of residents and their way of life back in the 19th century. An obvious respect and love for the Lone Star State permeates each of these restoration projects. The Bybee dream is that some day every county in Texas could have a living classroom of its heritage similar to the one she has endowed at Henkel Square.

Navarro House

228 S. Laredo Street
San Antonio 78207
512-226-4801
Hours: 10:00–4:00, Tues.–Sat.
Admission charge

About 1850 a prominent rancher and public official of the San Antonio area built a new house in town on the street known as Laredito. The house was typical of its time with thick walls of limestone, a pitched roof of cypress shingles that sloped gently to make a shady front gallery, and a shallow fireplace in each room to ward off the chilly winter northers. It stood in front of a long, low building which had been on the property from early Spanish times and later became the kitchen. Next to the new house was the *despacho* or office from which the family business was conducted.

Born in 1795 in San Antonio, Jose Antonio Navarro grew up in the atmosphere of revolution which swept across New Spain after the "Grito de Hidalgo" by Father Hidalgo in Mexico in 1810. Navarro's family was prominent in the local resistance to the corrupt power of Spain, and in 1813 young Jose Antonio was forced to flee into Louisiana. Returning after three years, the youth devoted himself to the study of business and law. When Mexico gained her independence, the

Jose Antonio Navarro made San Antonio his home after he and his uncle, Francisco Ruiz, became the only native-born Texans to sign the Texas Declaration of Independence.

Navarro fortunes increased, and Jose Antonio was elected to the legislature of the State of Coahuila and Texas in 1821.

Already fast friends with the American impresario, Stephen F. Austin, who was bringing Anglo-Americans into Texas, Navarro showed much sympathy for the aims and ambitions of these new colonists and became known as the "Americanized Texan." As events moved toward Texas independence, Navarro and his uncle, Francisco Ruiz, found themselves on the side of the Americans and against the dictator General Antonio Lopez de Santa Anna.

So, on March 2, 1836, after carefully weighing their old loyalty to their Mexican heritage against their sympathy and agreement with the Texas Revolution, both Jose Antonio Navarro and Francisco Ruiz signed the Texas Declaration of Independence. They were the only native-born Texans to sign this document.

In 1841, the Republic of Texas dispatched Navarro as a commissioner to accompany the foolhardy Santa Fe Expedition to New Mexico with the idea of convincing the citizens of the upper Rio Grande that their future lay with Texas rather than Mexico. The entire band of Texans was captured and marched thousands of grueling miles to prison in Mexico City.

Navarro was singled out for special pressure from Santa Anna because of his refusal to renounce his decision to cast his lot with a free Texas. Long after the other Texans were pardoned, Navarro was kept prisoner, first in Mexico City and later in Vera Cruz. Finally, the loyal Texan escaped to New Orleans and returned to his family in February of 1845. This was the Navarro that moved into the house on Laredito Street.

It wasn't easy to save the Navarro House. It took years for the San Antonio Conservation Society to acquire the necessary money to purchase the property and save it from destruction to make way for a new city-county jail. Old buildings all around the little Navarro house came tumbling down and sterile public buildings went up, but the historic compound was saved.

Finally, after three years of painstaking restoration, in October of 1964, the memorial to a great Texan was opened as a museum. On display, along with the Declarations of Independence of Texas and the United States, is the famous "Grito de Hidalgo" of Mexico, a fitting tribute to Jose Antonio Navarro.

Spanish Governor's Palace

More than 200 years ago this white-plastered adobe building with its 3-foot-thick walls may have seemed somewhat palatial compared to the other crude huts in San Antonio in 1722. Now, it is all that remains of the old Spanish presidio established under the orders of the Marquis of San Miguel de Aguayo, governor general of the New Philippines. The Hapsburg coat of arms above the front doors of the palace bears the date 1749, and historians believe this was the date the structure was officially dedicated.

The Governor's Palace actually evolved from the establishment of the Presidio de San Antonio de Bexar built for the protection of the Mission San Antonio de

105 Military Plaza
San Antonio 78205
512-224-0601
Hours: 9:00–5:00, Mon.–Sat.
10:00–5:00, Sun.
Admission charge

The Spanish Governor's Palace was part of the Presidio de San Antonio de Bexar built for the protection of the Mission San Antonio de Valero, better known as the Alamo.

Valero, better known as the Alamo. Originally the Comandancia, the Governor's Palace was the residence of the captain of the presidio. When San Antonio became the capital of the Spanish Province of Texas, the Spanish governors took up residence, thus giving rise to the name Governor's Palace, a rather elegant name for a plain adobe building.

By 1821, when Mexico won her independence, 32 Spanish governors had lived in the house. They had entertained a variety of famous people in the Palace, one of whom was the learned Father Agustin Morfi, a distinguished early Texas writer. Father Morfi complained that his quarters were cramped and the sentinel kept him awake blowing the bugle.

American explorer Captain Zebulon Pike was lavishly wined and dined in the Palace in 1807. During the day Pike attended conferences with Governors Cordero and Herrera, and at night he danced with the beauties of San Antonio.

One visitor did not receive such a warm welcome. In fact, he was not received at all and ordered to leave San Antonio immediately. Moses Austin's great plan for Texas came terribly close to complete failure, but it was saved by the intervention of an old friend, Baron de Bastrop, a confidant of the Spanish governor. (See "Friend of the Empresarios," *Unsung Heroes of Texas*, Lone Star Books, Houston, 1986.)

Folk hero Jim Bowie was such a welcome guest to the Governor's Palace, he courted and married Governor Veramendi's daughter, Ursula, in 1831. Two years later Bowie introduced another legendary Texan to Governor Veramendi, and Sam Houston was entertained royally.

After the capture of San Antonio in 1835, the Palace was the headquarters for all the Alamo heroes, as well as for Colonel Seguin who, after the battle of San Jacinto, gathered up the ashes of the martyrs of the Alamo and took them to the Palace to lie in state.

Despite its grand and exciting history, the palace fell into decay. It became a school, a restaurant, a second-hand clothing store and even a bar called "The Hole in the Wall." Finally, a movement began to save the historic Palace, and in 1929 the city purchased the Palace from the granddaughter of Jose Ignacio Perez, the man who had obtained it back in 1804.

In 1929 the restoration of the Palace cost approximately $30,000 and was such a success that even today experts find it difficult to distinguish between where the old leaves off and the new begins. The hand-hewn timbers in the ceiling are really old decaying telephone poles the Public Service Company contributed from their scrap pile. Some of the wrought iron lamps are more than 200 years old, yet the rest are reproductions.

The Palace is furnished in a combination of richly carved Spanish antiques and simple colonial pieces, most of them bearing a plaque with their donor's name. The single piece of furniture which draws the most attention is the carved rosewood bed in the main bedroom. Of Flemish design, its carved spiral posts and headboard are a work of art. Several pieces in the Palace were selected by art expert Vincent Price, to be reproduced nationally.

Outside of the Palace is a handsome statue of a Spanish Conquistador. This unique and appropriate gift was a gift from Spain when the restoration was completed.

The Palace has many many ghost stories and legends of buried treasure. In fact, the patio was torn to shreds by seekers of hidden gold. Now it is a lovely spot for weddings and receptions completely protected by thick walls from the roar of San Antonio traffic.

The Spanish Governor's Palace is one of the rare buildings from the reign of Colonial Spain still standing in Texas. Its excellent restoration and preservation make it one of Texas' most significant shrines to its Spanish heritage.

(See color photo.)

Steves Homestead

Texans always like to boast of their state's "firsts." And, one important "first" is that San Antonio's King William District was first district in the United States to be placed on the National Register of Historic Places. That was back in 1967, and great changes have taken place since then. Loving hands that held fat pocketbooks have transformed seedy and run-down wrecks of old mansions into elegant and gracious homes just as they were at the turn of the century.

When Ernst Altgelt was naming the streets of this new subdivision back in the late 1800s, he honored his Old World heritage by naming a main thoroughfare Wilhelm I for the King of Prussia. It rapidly became anglicized to King William, and here were built the homes of San Antonio's rich and powerful citizens. The area was also crudely referred to as "Sauerkraut Bend" because of its large number of German inhabitants.

One of the leading citizens of King William was German immigrant Edward Steves. He built his handsome and imposing Victorian home in 1876 for $12,000 after making his fortune in the lumber and building business. Edward died in 1890, and his wife, Johanna, lived here until her death 39 years later. Even though the house was then rented, it escaped the usual dismal fate of such houses of being divided into apartments. Johanna's granddaughter, Edna Steves Vaughn, graciously donated her family home to the San Antonio Conservation Society in 1952.

509 King William Street
San Antonio 78205
512-225-5924
Hours: 10:00–5:00, daily
Admission charge

The ornate Steves Homestead is in San Antonio's King William District, once known as "Sauerkraut Bend" for its numerous German residents.

Constructed of ashlar limestone, the house features a slate-covered mansard roof and iron cresting. Originally lighted with gas, the Steves Homestead was the first house in San Antonio to have electricity installed.

As was often the fashion in homes of this era, the woodwork was ordered out of a catalog, as were the parlor's pocket doors with their beautiful etched glass panels. The handsome newel post cost $11.00, and the very ornate statue posed majestically atop was a souvenir of the Steves' trip to the nation's centennial. Johanna had it converted to a light fixture.

The Steves lived in a gorgeous mansion, but Johanna was still a frugal haus frau. Her dining room chairs cost a paltry $1.75 each, yet each bedroom had the luxury of a basin with running water. Even if it was only one faucet for cold water, it was still an expensive fixture. Also, another real luxury was that each of the four bedrooms had a closet. Since houses were taxed on the number of rooms, and a closet was considered a room, no matter how small, the Steves home was truly first class. Note that there are no racks in the closets, only hooks. Coat hangers had not been invented yet.

No drafty, dirty fireplaces for Johanna, the Steves heated their home with free-standing stoves. And she was one of the first to acquire that wonderful invention—steam heating.

A really unique addition in 1910 to this grand old house was Johanna's natatorium. In her enclosed swimming pool, this active lady swam every day until her death at age 92. The natatorium was floored in to provide a meeting room for the Society, but the artesian well which Johanna dug in protest to the high cost of city water service is still used today to water the grounds.

The Steves Homestead is King William's only house museum open to the public on a regular basis, and it is an outstanding example of the opulence which graced San Antonio in another age.

(See color photo.)

Lyndon Johnson's Birthplace

LBJ was born in the Hill Country of central Texas, a land whose people survived harsh weather and hostile Indians to produce new generations of Texas/Americans with a strength arising from a common-sense philosophy and a hard-work ethic. From this background came Lyndon Baines Johnson, the nation's 36th president, who took Washington by storm with boundless energy and a determination to get things done. His frontier roots helped him bridge the gap between the old rural America of his youth and the new America of world power and sophistication he eventually led. Outside Johnson City, the life of one of Texas' favorite sons has been memorialized with a National Park where visitors may tour his reconstructed birthplace house, restored boyhood home, and a living history farm.

The modest tree-shaded house where the President was born was rebuilt and furnished by the Johnsons as a guest house before they donated their property in this area for a national park. (The quilt covering one bed was made by Johnson's great-grandmother before the Civil War.) You can take a short walk from the birthplace down to the banks of the Pedernales River where a simple headstone designates the President's grave. Near the visitor's center you see the President's boyhood home where Sam and Rebekah Johnson, great believers in education, taught some of their children's lessons. The family would gather in the dining room and listen to speeches on the big-belled Atwater Kent radio. Sam Johnson embellished his children's education by asking them to analyze the content of the speech, and his wife ordered critiques of the delivery.

An additional treat in the LBJ Park is the Sauer-Beckman Living History Farm where visitors learn how a Hill Country farm operated in the early years of this century. Naturally no power or telephones are around, and day-to-day chores are performed by park staff who wear period clothing and use authentic turn-of-the-century tools. Life at the farmstead is depicted as it was lived in LBJ's formative years. In the space of one afternoon, visitors to the National Park and ranch complex can trace Johnson's entire life from birth through boyhood and from his presidency to the final days on the ranch in the state and near the people from which he came.

(See color photo.)

LBJ State Park
Box 238
Stonewall 78671
512-644-2252
Hours: 9:00–5:00, Memorial Day to
Labor Day
8:00–4:00, remainder of the
year
Accessible only by park tour
bus from LBJ State Park,
14 miles west of Johnson
City on US290.
Free admission

Earle-Harrison House

Who could look at the stately Earle-Harrison House with its elegant cypress columns and imagine they are seeing only half a house? When Dr. and Mrs. Baylis Wood Earle began construction on their elegant two story home in 1858, they planned a house of pure Greek Renaissance design, encircled by four galleries and two-story cypress columns. The doctor's untimely death a year later halted plans for the remainder of the mansion, so what we see today is half that dream. Nonetheless, the Earle-Harrison House commands admiration for its beauty and respect for the quality of materials that allowed it to survive two moves and over a

1901 North Fifth St.
Waco 76708
817-753-2032
Hours: By appointment
Admission charge

century of living. Cypress siding was used to construct the exterior along with handmade bricks from the Earle plantation. (Hand and chicken feet imprints remain in the bricks.) The heart-of-pine flooring was brought from near Houston and the nine great cypress columns came overland by oxen from east Texas. All windows were designed to be used as doors to the galleries, six feet tall (people were shorter then) and wide enough to accommodate the ladies' skirt hoops.

Dr. Earle came to Texas from Mississippi where he had already made a fortune in cotton before the land "wore out." On the advice of a relative, he moved to the virgin land of Texas outside Marlin where he built two more plantations. His home, however, was always in Waco. With cotton flourishing again, the doctor practiced medicine only for those from whom he accepted no fee—friends, family, and slaves. Several years following her husband's death, Mrs. Earle sold the house to her brother, Confederate General Thomas Harrison. By this time Waco surrounded the Harrison house, but the street passed by its short end. Not wanting his home to seem dwarfed, General Harrison jacked the two-story mansion up on logs and used mules to move it fifty yards where its longer and more attractive side was visible to those passing by.

The old home's detached kitchen contains the Gov. Pat Neff collection of Texas kitchen utensils, courtesy of the governor's daughter, Hallie Maude Harrison Wilcox. And inside are many old family pieces the Earles brought overland from Mississippi. A marble topped pier table still retains its original spot in the entrance hall. The middle parlor has two Victorian sofas, a square grand piano, and two balloon back chairs that also came from Mississippi. Silver pieces in the dining room are original as are the Duncan Fife and Hepplewhite tables.

In 1968 the G. H. Pape Foundation moved the house to its present location and completed its restoration by adding a lovely lily pond and fountain to embellish the garden side. A visit to the historic Earle-Harrison House offers not only a romantic visit to the antebellum South but the added treat of water and flower gardens that refresh the spirit, warm the heart, and entreat visitors to return again.

(See color photo.)

East Terrace

100 Mill St.
Waco 76707
817-753-5166
Hours: 2:00–5:00, Sat. and Sun.
Admission charge

Most of Texas' historic homes were built by pioneers who emigrated from the South where Greek Revival or Victorian architecture was preferred. However, John Wesley Mann from Tennessee bowed to his wife's Hudson River background and chose an Italianate Villa design for their home, East Terrace. The style features small, cozy rooms and a tower where the owner could look out over his cotton plantation and brick business. The smaller rooms were easier to heat but probably a bit uncomfortable in the summer. Unlike the Hudson, the unruly Brazos River overran its banks a bit too often, and the house was under water up to the second floor gallery at least seven times. During the 1913 flood Mrs. Mann refused to leave until her favorite cow was taken up to the second floor, safe from the rising waters. Now that the river is under control and the house climatized, the delicate Italianate design with its thin, vertical proportions adds a lovely silhouette to the drive along the Brazos.

The Italiante Villa design used for East Terrace was most unusual for its time in early Texas.

Among John Mann's enterprises was his brick business. Some of the most perfect bricks, of natural river and sand colors, were set aside for use in his house, terraces, storm cellar, and chimneys. Every room in East Terrace had a fireplace with the exception of the dining room and one bedroom. Estimates are that two full-time servants were needed to keep the fireplaces going continuously. The Manns enlarged their home several times; the second addition, designed for entertaining, contained a second-story ballroom with its own entrance. Long shuttered windows and arches open to the second story gallery where the orchestra would sometimes sit on the front balcony.

East Terrace contains some pieces of furniture original to the house and a few of significant repute. Mrs. Mann's small Victorian secretary, rocker, and bamboo chairs are in the sitting room, and Mr. Mann's portrait from his bank hangs above the mantle. Mrs. Mann's copy of *The Scarlet Letter* rests on a desk used at one time by Sam Houston in a business he ran in Houston. Ladies of Waco placed antique umbrellas on the handsome walnut hall tree, and above a chest in the family sitting room hangs a portrait of Robert E. Lee. Most Southern families displayed a picture of their beloved general. The chandelier was originally in the home of Gov. Pat M. Neff.

This delicately stylish old home was named East Terrace because originally its grounds were terraced at intervals with brick walls and walks down to the river. Rose gardens, strutting peacocks, a sunken garden with a goldfish pond, an orchard, and columbine draped terraces contributed to the grandeur that could be viewed from the galleries and tower above. The elegant grounds failed to survive the test of time, but the East Terrace Villa has weathered floods, additions, and renovations. Her delicate facade conceals the 110-year-old stout heart of one of Waco's outstanding historic ladies.

Fort House

503 South 4th
Waco 76707
817-753-5166
Hours: 2:00–5:00, Sat. and Sun.
Admission charge

The stately Greek Revival home of Colonel W. A. Fort was built in 1868 during post Civil War Reconstruction years. The Forts were a family of means at the time their Waco house was constructed, but the early years had not been easy ones. At age 28 William Fort and a friend traveled to this area of Texas from Alabama in search of good farming country. Liking what they found, the young men returned to Alabama and set out for Waco with an entourage of five hundred families and slaves in oxcarts and mule-drawn wagons. The caravan arrived six rigorous weeks later in April 1854.

William Fort established a large plantation about four miles south of Waco and married two years later. By the time the Confederacy called William Fort to duty, the family had increased to six. Mrs. Fort managed the plantation while her husband was fighting for the Confederacy; in the meantime the Forts became guardians to two nephews and a niece whose parents died. After the war, the Colonel thought it would be too difficult to manage a large plantation without slaves, so he decided to move into town and enter business. Their new home, known as Fort House, was built and the seven children, parents, and a grandmother moved in.

In the beginning, a perfect balance of Greek Revival style was used for the exterior. Soon, however, the size and needs of the family called for modification, and in 1872 the house was enlarged to provide more storage and work space at the back. Out of this effort the kitchen was attached to the house and a pantry was built with provisions kept under lock and key. Like other ladies of large houses, Mrs. Fort wore a great ring of keys. Each morning she dished out provisions for the day—flour, sugar, coffee—and kept check of the inventory to be certain there was enough; it took a lot to feed a large family and servants. Though Colonel Fort

Col. William Fort built this home near the center of Waco where it served as a hub of social activity after the Civil War.

was a great provider, he never bought anything he could grow on his plantation. Some say he bought only tea and coffee.

The lively Fort family used the parlors of their home for many happy times. Here Colonel Fort served the first iced punch in Waco at the coming out party of his daughter May. Here also the daughters entertained only the young men who had been "approved." Any suitor who wished to call sent a note to the Colonel's place of business and waited for a reply giving his approval. In the back parlor hangs a gilt-framed mirror, the only furnishing original to the house. Two interesting portraits adorn the dining room, an enlarged tinted photo of Colonel Fort and one of his only daughter, May, who died of typhoid in 1878.

Colonel Fort prospered as a business man and was respected as a good manager and loving father. Strict attention was given to the children's education and training. Because the Colonel believed young men should be taught to assume responsibility for their actions, living quarters were arranged so that the boys' bedroom allowed the five young men freedom to go and return as they chose without observation. Apparently the girls were not expected to learn personal responsibility; theirs was the only room that did not open onto the gallery.

Colonel Fort died at the age of 52, only one month after the death of his beloved daughter. In his short life time, he migrated to Texas, raised a family, fought in a war, and returned to promote business and education for the future. His industrious determination and foresight, like many other pioneers', was a building block in the structure of Texas. Wacoans take pride in the Fort family who contributed to their city's foundation and in the house that stands as a memorial to their efforts.

McCullough House

One of the most interesting architectural achievements among the historic homes of Waco is the Greek Revival style home known as the McCullough House. On this spot in 1867, Josiah Caldwell built a two room cabin and detached kitchen for his wife and children. They lived in the house only four years before selling it for $6,000 in gold to the Champe McCullough family who immediately enlarged the house to the noble-looking two-story structure still in existence today. The McCulloughs raised seven children here, and one or more member of the family resided in the house until 1971, exactly one century. Records show that Champe Sr. served in the Civil War, was in the grocery business, and sold insurance for a time. He was mayor of Waco from 1890 until 1900 and died of a stroke in 1907.

Today little remains in the house that belonged to the McCulloughs. An old family bible, a gift from Champe to his wife, is displayed on a table in the salon; therein births and deaths are recorded. Each daughter was given a silver tea service, and one of them was generously returned to its historic home courtesy of a Waco family. It is on display in the dining room.

406 Columbus Ave.
Waco 76707
817-753-5166
Hours: 2:00–5:00, Sat. and Sun.
Closed December
Admission charge

Waco's McCullough House grew from a two-room cabin to the Greek Revival home of to-day. It was occupied 100 years by the same family.

The children's education was a matter of extremes; most of them never finished more than the eighth or ninth grades. However, one daughter, Sally, received music training and performed at a music conservatory in Los Angeles. (The school only existed for two years.) She went to Europe during World War I, contributed to the war effort, and married before returning home. Another of the daughters also had music training. Then there was the oldest son, Champe Carter McCullough, Jr., who apparently enjoyed the academic world, because he earned a civil engineering degree from Texas A and M, a medical degree from the University of Virginia, and was awarded an honorary Ph.D. from Baylor. Interestingly enough, Baylor did not have a doctoral program at that time, so we can only speculate how they were able to award this degree. Apparently hard times fell on the McCulloughs after the father died, because Mrs. McCullough took in boarders and two of the daughters returned home to live and teach music lessons.

Thanks to generous benefactors in Waco, this home contains a lovely and historically noteworthy painting. The subject is a child making lace. The child in the painting is Ann Pamela Cunningham, the lady who led the committee to restore Mt. Vernon. Another unusual piece is the landlord's table, a rotating round table of drawers. In each drawer papers were kept relating to a different tenant, and naturally every drawer could be locked. Upstairs you can see the McCulloughs' marriage certificate, a photo of Mrs. McCullough, and a note from Champe asking if he could call on her.

During the century the McCullough family possessed this house, several of the children moved in and out for periods of time. With the death of the last daughter-in-law, the house stood empty for several years during which time it was heavily vandalized. After months of unrelenting effort by Mr. John B. McNamara and Mrs. Maurice Barnes, Historic Waco Foundation acquired and restored the home which they open on weekends for touring. Festive decorations greet those who take time to see McCullough House during the Christmas On The Brazos celebration. Or for those who enjoy spring outings, see the home during the Brazos River Festival.

The Anson Jones Home

For a time the Republic of Texas' capital was located at Washington-on-the-Brazos, a lovely spot atop a gently rolling rise in the Texas Hill Country. It was here that Anson Jones, fourth and last president, took his oath of office to the Texas Republic and managed its foreign affairs prior to annexation by the United States in 1846. His early life, however, scarcely seems an appropriate prelude for his tragic end. Anson Jones secured his medical diploma in 1827 and practiced medicine in Philadelphia, Venezuela, and New Orleans. In 1833 he arrived by ship in Brazoria, Texas with $17 in his pocket and the intention to practice medicine. Though he supported himself as a doctor, he soon involved himself in activities to benefit the new territory he called home. He obtained the charter for the first Masonic Lodge in Texas in 1835, helped frame the first constitution of Texas in 1836, and then served in the Texas army as a surgeon.

Following Texas' independence, Anson Jones became judge advocate general and in 1837 was elected to congress where he advocated medical legislation, establishment of uniform education under Congress, and the dedication of public lands for endowment of a university. He also urged advertising Texas' potential to foreign nations. After holding several other important political posts, Jones was elected fourth president of the Republic of Texas. As president he managed the foreign affairs of the Republic until he completed the last formalities of annexation to the United States in 1846.

By 1845 Jones had built a house on his plantation at Barrington near Brenham. The house was constructed of local cedar wood in the typical dog trot design with an upstairs sleeping loft for his boys. In preparation for the Texas Centennial, the house was divided and moved to the Washington-on-the-Brazos State Park in 1936, but it was left untouched and eventually became a storehouse for hay. Res-

P. O. Box 305
Washington 77880
409-878-2214
Hours: 10:00–5:00, daily
Admission charge

The home of Anson Jones, fourth and last president of the Republic of Texas, sits atop a gently rolling rise at Washington-on-the-Brazos. The house reflects the simplicity of plantation life in Texas at that time.

toration finally began in 1967. Then in 1976 the Texas Parks and Wildlife Department acquired the house and completed its restoration. Some parlor furnishings are original. A photograph of Jones hangs over the parlor mantle, and an 1860 photo of Mary Jones and the children greets guests in the dog trot. The furniture in the bedroom, from France, was given by the French Ambassador.

Only six years after building his house, Anson Jones suffered an injury that rendered one of his arms useless. For seven years morphine barely enabled him to live with the pain. Jones' motives had been greatly misunderstood when as the last President of the Republic he had tried to offer Texans a clear choice between annexation to Mexico and statehood with the United States. It was clearly the confusion over this issue that caused him to lose a senatorial bid in 1857. Bitterly disappointed when he lost the election and suffering constantly with his lame arm, Jones shot himself in the old Capitol Hotel in Houston, the building where he first had served as senator. His widow, Mary, lived in Harris County until her death in 1907 and left her own mark on Texas history by helping organize the Daughters of the Republic of Texas and serving as its first president.

At one time Anson Jones possessed so much respect for his fellow patriot, Sam Houston, that he named his oldest son Sam Houston Jones. In later years, however, the enmity between the two men became so intense that Jones renamed his son Samuel Edward Jones and said, "You will never again carry the Villain of Texas' Name." Ironically, both of these heroes, who had given so much of themselves and their lives to the Republic, died in bitter disappointment with their final role in Texas history.

McGregor-Grimm House

Winedale
Contact: Winedale Historical Center
P.O. Box 11
Round Top, Texas 78954
409-278-3530
Hours: May–Oct.: 10:00–6:00, Sat.,
12:00–6:00, Sun.
Nov.-April: 9:00–5:00, Sat.,
12:00–5:00, Sun.

Admission charge

Nestled in the rolling hills of South Central Texas, tiny Winedale has been a part of the Lone Star's history a long, long time. One of Austin's original colonists, William S. Townsend, was granted 190 acres here in 1831. Townsend sold his farmstead in 1848 to Samuel Lewis, and by the mid-1850s the farm was a popular stop on the well-traveled stage road between La Grange and Brenham.

Winedale, named for the abundance of grapevines in the area, was finally purchased in 1961 by the well-known Houston philanthropist, Miss Ima Hogg. This true lover of Texas' heritage carried out an extensive restoration and donated the entire historic complex to the University of Texas.

Winedale offers a trip back in time to those pioneer days before and after the Revolution. And, one of the main attractions of this quaint collection of Texana is the McGregor-Grimm House. This two-story Greek Revival farmhouse was built in 1861 by a Washington County planter and land speculator, Dr. Gregor McGregor, for his bride, Anna Portia Fordtran.

The house was originally constructed in Wesley, about 15 miles to the east of Winedale, but in 1967 Miss Ima had the home moved to its new site. To retain its authenticity, the house was relocated in an identical grove of trees and shrubbery, and a pond dug nearby, just as it was in Wesley.

Here at the McGregor-Grimm House you find an excellent example of the life-style of wealthy Anglo-German families of the 1860s. As you enter the center hallway, note the hand-painted Greek columns on the walls. Wallpaper was a rare luxury, even for the well-to-do, and painted walls were the vogue. Several of the rooms of this handsome manse are decorated with excellent wall-paintings by Rudolf Melchior. Another trend of this era was to paint plain wood to resemble expensive stone. The parlor's mantle is actually pine, but at a casual glance it appears to be marble.

Furnishings of this fine old home are authentic to the period, such as the horse-hair sofa with its hand-carved fish trim on the back. Wedding wreaths were popular during the 1800s, and to commemorate 25th and 50th anniversaries, couples often remarried. The bride wore a silver or gold wreath and the husband a boutonniere. Then, these treasured tokens were framed and hung in the parlor.

Miss Ima put many fine antiques in this charming restoration, but one of the most delightful is a series of nine hand-carved shadow boxes. These rough-hewn gimcracks depict the Bible story of Jacob and his coat of many colors.

Walk out on the balcony of the second story and note how the Texas Star has been carefully trimmed out of the boxwood hedge on the lawn, and the teardrop drive is identical to the drive the house had in Wesley.

Miss Ima has assembled several other historic buildings in the Winedale complex and created a quaint and charming segment of Texas' past.

OTHER
NOTEWORTHY HOMES

Northeast and East Texas

Daniel House
107 East Bluff
Granbury 76048
817-573-5548
Hours: By appointment
    Admission charge

Granbury proudly offers tours of the Daniel House, a Victorian home occupied exclusively by the family of the same name. It has a total of ten rooms, including five bedrooms and a double parlor. Several of the original light bulbs in the house are still in use.

(See color photo.)

The Captain's Castle
403 E. Walker
Jefferson 75657
214-665-7317
Hours: 9:30–4:00, daily
    Admission charge

Mr. and Mrs. A. B. Bradley have restored and furnished their colorful home which now beckons visitors who appreciate extraordinary examples of antique stitchery and handwork. Musical strains from an antique Victrola set a delightful mood to enjoy the old home's history.

Governor Hogg Cottage
Old Stinson Home
Rt. 3
Quitman 75783
214-763-2701
Hours: 9:00–12;00, 1:00–4:00,
    Wed.–Sun.
    Admission charge

The Governor Hogg Shrine State Historical Park has two family homes open for touring—Governor and Mrs. Hogg's first home, the one known as the Honeymoon Cottage, and Mrs. Hogg's family residence, the Old Stinson Home. Each house contains an outstanding array of period antiques collected in Europe by Miss Ima Hogg.

The Gulf Coast

Charles Stillman House
   1305 Washington
   Brownsville
   512-542-2392
   Hours: 10:00–12:00, 2:00–5:00,
      Mon.–Fri.
      Donations requested

Almost overwhelmed by downtown stores is this gracious Greek Revival home built in 1850, just two years after the fledgling river-frontier town of Brownsville was laid out by Charles Stillman. Note the bricks in the walk marked "US." They are from the original Fort Brown constructed in 1848.

(See color photo.)

Monroe-Crook House
   709 East Houston Ave.
   Crockett 75835
   409-544-2473 or 544-3616
   Hours: 9:30–11:30, Wed.
      2:00–4:00, Sat.–Sun.
      Admission charge

Here in the first county formed under the new Republic of Texas is the 1854 Monroe-Crook House. It was built by Armistead Thompson Mason Monroe, grand nephew of James Monroe, fifth president of the United States and referred to as "one of the finest early Greek Revival houses in Texas."

Moore House
   406 S. Fifth
   Richmond 77469
   713-342-6478
   Hours: 1:00–5:00, Sun.
      Admission charge

Moore House began its existence as in the Victorian Gothic style, but U.S. Congressman John M. Moore decided his 1883 home was hardly elegant enough for their social status and completely remodeled the house to its present Greek Revival style in 1905.

Davison Home
   109 Third Avenue North
   Texas City 77590
   409-948-3111
   Hours: 1:00–4:00, First Sunday of
      each month
      Admission charge

Just a few short blocks from the bay stands a grand old survivor of the devastating 1900 storm and also the 1947 blast of the ship *Grandcamp* that left a death toll of 576—the Frank Davison Home. Built in 1897, this historic home is now the center of many Texas City social functions.

West and Central Texas

Kraitchar House
> P.O. Box 127
> Caldwell 77836
> House: 2:00–5:00, Sun.
>> Donations requested

Many fine old homes grace Caldwell's shady streets, but this classic Victorian cottage built in 1891 is typical of the homes of many industrious and hard-working Texas immigrants. Far from magnificent, the Kraitchar House is still a delight to visit.

Waverly Plantation
> Drawer E
> Chappell Hill 77426
> 409-836-5067
> Hours: By appointment
>> Admission charge

This gracious Greek Revival antebellum house was built about 1850 and probably named for the popular Walter Scott Waverly novels. Furnished with beautiful antiques, it is a highlight on the Chappel Hill Historic Homes Tours.

(See color photo.)

S. W. Lowe House
> P.O. Box 1250
> Clarendon 79226
> 806-874-3332
> Hours: By appointment
>> Admission charge

To capture an unforgettable and beautiful memory of life on the prairie shortly after the turn of the century, take a guided tour through the S. W. Lowe house. Owner Zell SoRelle has meticulously restored the old Victorian house featuring five bays and a multiplaned gable roof.

Earle-Napier-Kinnard House
> 814 South 4th St.
> Waco 76707
> 817-753-5166
> Hours: 2:00–5:00, Sat. and Sun.
>> Admission charge

The Earle-Napier-Kinnard House sits beside a bustling interstate freeway. It looks just as at home in its present setting as it did beside an unpaved road more than a hundred years ago. The neo-classic architecture and elegant furnishings of this newly restored home make it a must for your Waco visit.

ANNUAL HISTORIC HOME TOURS

FEBRUARY

Wichita Falls—Kell House Valentine
   Party and Sale
Valentine's Day
817-723-0623

MARCH

Brenham
Last weekend
Heritage Home Tours
409-836-3695

APRIL

Anderson's Texas Trek
First weekend
409-825-6600

Cuero Tour of Homes
First weekend
512-275-2112

Llano Historical Tour
Second weekend
915-247-5354

Victoria Historical Homes Tour
Second weekend
512-573-5277

Montgomery Trek Home Tour
Third Sunday
Montgomery Historical Society
409-597-6304

Rusk County Tourist Development
   Department Home Tour
Third weekend
409-369-4311

San Antonio King William Tour of
   Homes
Third Saturday
512-227-8786

Sherman Past and Present
Third weekend
214-892-9091

San Marcos Portraits Past and Present
Last weekend
512-396-3739

Waco—Brazos River Festival
Last weekend
817-753-5166

Weatherford—Sharing our Legacy
Fourth weekend
817-594-3801

Belton Historical Homes Tour
Last weekend in April and first weekend
   in May
817-939-2169

MAY

Fort Worth Urban Pioneer Home Tour
First weekend
817-926-9102

Galveston Annual Historic Homes Tour
First weekend
409-762-8687

Navasota Nostalgia Days
First weekend
409-825-6600

Columbus, Magnolia Homes Tour, Inc.
Third weekend
713-732-5881

JUNE

San Augustine Annual Tour of Homes
   and Historical Places
First weekend
409-275-3610

Waxahachie Gingerbread Trail
First weekend
214-937-0681

JULY

Wichita Falls
Kell House July 4th Celebration
817-723-0623

SEPTEMBER

Castroville Pilgrimage
Last weekend (every other year)
512-538-3142

Dallas—Oak Cliffs Historic Homes Tour
Last weekend
214-948-1280

OCTOBER

Caldwell—Make Mine Country
First Saturday
409-567-3218

Crockett Fall Festival
First weekend
409-544-4804

Gonzales Tour of Homes
First weekend
512-672-2514

Marlin Tour of Historic Places
Early October
817-883-2171

Winnsboro Historic Tour of Homes
Late October
214-342-3666

NOVEMBER

Marshall—Ghosts of Christmas Past
   Candlelight Tour
Late November
214-935-7868

DECEMBER

Richmond—A Colonial Christmas on
   the Brazos
Early December
Fort Bend County Museum
409-342-6478

Beaumont—Candlelight Tour
John Jay French Museum
First Saturday
409-898-0348

Caldwell Christmas Homes Tour
First Saturday
409-567-3218

Cleburne Candlelight Walk
First Saturday
817-645-2455

Granbury Candlelight Tour of Homes
First Saturday
817-573-5548

Bryan Historic Homes Tour
First weekend
409-260-9898

Fort Worth (Park Hill) Christmas on the
   Hill
First weekend
817-624-2765

Fort Worth (Ryan Place) Candlelight
   Tour
First weekend
817-927-7580

Goliad—Christmas in Goliad
First weekend
512-645-3479

Waco—Christmas on the Brazos
First weekend
817-753-5166

Henderson Christmas Candlelight Tour
Mid-December
Howard-Dickinson House
214-657-6925

Jefferson Christmas Candlelight Tour
First weekend
214-665-8880

Stonewall—LBJ State Park Christmas Party
Lady Bird Johnson selects the evening and lights the tree.
512-644-2252

McKinney Christmas Tour of Homes
First weekend
214-542-2560

Salado County Christmas weekend
First weekend
812-947-5567

Missouri City—Heaven on Earth Candlelight Tour
Mid-December
713-499-1840

Bastrop Christmas Tour of Homes
Second weekend
512-321-9717

Dallas (Winnetka Heights)
Second weekend
214-948-1280

Fredericksburg Kristkindl Market and Candlelight Tour of Homes
Second weekend
512-997-6523

Galveston—Spirit of Christmas
Second weekend
409-765-7834

Montgomery Christmas in Old Montgomery Home Tour
Second weekend of December
409-597-6304

Paris Christmas at the Maxey House
Mid-December
214-785-5716

Rusk Area Christmas Tour of Homes
Early December
409-369-4311

Tomball Candlelight Tour of the Griffin House
Second weekend in December
713-351-4244

Wichita Falls—Kell House Christmas Party
Mid-December
817-723-0623

Big Springs Christmas Tour of Homes
Near Christmas time.
915-263-7641

ALL YEAR

Bellville—A Day in the Country
Four homes of historic interest and luncheon
Highcotton Tours
409-865-9796

❖ INDEX ❖